Ever wonder what Key W
pages?

Behind closed doors?

Ever been curious about what naughtiness all those celebrities get up to when they're down here on the rock?

Want to learn more about our charismatic local celebrities?

Get ready for some eye-popping facts and just a grain of gagging dirt and sexy scandal.

Pull up a barstool and order your favorite vice. Let's get this party started.

**BTW: Since a picture is worth a 1000 words—perhaps more nowadays, what with inflation—I've sprinkled the narrative with some links to a slew of righteous videos and the odd photo—available online. (For those of you who don't read on Kindle or other eReaders, feel free to pay a visit to my website where the links will all be duly listed at the bottom of the homepage: www.JonBreakfield.com).

WHY DIDN'T YOU JUST PUT THE BLEEPING PHOTOS IN THE BOOK? you ask.

Good question!

Sadly, the price of the book would have quadrupled, and I didn't want to cut into any of your good beer money.

The following Fact Book is an enlightening and plucky departure from my traditional KEY WEST SERIES fayre.

BTW again: What? What's that you ask? *When is* **KEY WEST BOOK #5 *coming?*

Well, am I ever glad you asked. I'm working on it as we speak, and you will be the first to know when I have the book launch.

"Don't bother with churches, government buildings or city squares. If you want to know about a culture, spend a night in its bars"—**Ernest Hemingway**

"Key West is an insane asylum. We're just too lazy to put up the walls or fences. I want to retain that mystique"—**Former Mayor of Key West Capt. Tony**

"In Key West, it's sometimes hard to tell the good guys from the bad guys"—**Johnny-Johnny**

"If I didn't live here, I couldn't afford to come down and visit"—**Tom Luna**

"Be yourself, no one can ever tell you you're doing it wrong—**James Leo Herlihy, author of *The Midnight Cowboy***

"Everybody has problems, and the thing is to function despite these problems and to be a nice person and a good person and a functional creative but a productive person in spite of the problems you have. We all have hang-ups"—**Shel Silverstein**

"Every outlaw has a good story, and Jimmy Buffett has an eye and ear for them"—**Bob Anderson, *High Times***

"I need chaos … I have a mortal fear of being housebroken"—**Tom McGuane**

"Die doin' what you love"—**Shel Silverstein**

"If you don't like to read, you haven't found the right book"—**Key West Island Bookstore**

SLOTH-LIKE DISCLAIMER:

THIS BOOK WAS TEN YEARS IN THE MAKING (don't ask) **AND IS PENNED FOR ALL WHO LIVE ON THE ROCK, ALL WHO VISIT, AND ALL OF YOU WHO ARE BENT ON AN ALCOHOL-FUELED ONE-NIGHT STAND, BUT END UP SPENDING A LONG LONELY NIGHT IN OUR LOCAL POKEY INSTEAD.**

You know who you are…

ABOUT THE AUTHOR

Jon Breakfield is a former TV writer (*Trapper John, M.D.*, and ABC After School Specials) and the author of nine books.

These include the Amazon bestsellers:

KEY WEST: Tequila, a Pinch of Salt and a Quirky Slice of America (first in the Key West Series)

KEY WEST: Part II (the Seagull, I mean the Sequel)

KEY WEST: Starting Over (third in the series)

KEY WEST: See It Before It Sinks (fourth in the series)

PAN AM: No Sex Please, We're Flight Attendants (much laughter, much sorrow)

NAKED EUROPE (naughty and mildly erotic)

DEATH by GLASGOW (gritty crime thriller)

DEATH by KEY WEST (crime thriller and stand-alone sequel to the above)

LIVERPOOL, TEXAS … LONDON, ARKANSAS (short story, short attention span required)

Jon and his wife divide their time between drinking beer and drinking wine… Wait! That came out wrong. I mean to say Jon and his wife divide their time between the cobblestoned-streets of Glasgow, Scotland, and the quaint tropical lanes of Key West, FL, not quite the USA, just there at the end of the line.

KEY WEST

Celebrities

&

A SPLASH OF SCANDAL

by

Jon Breakfield

KW
Press

To Suzanne Hughes Orchard, Paul Orchard, and the team at the Key West Island Bookstore

ACKNOWLEDGEMENTS AND MANY THANKS TO: **Will and Amy Soto, Baby Tracy and the Fabulous Spectrelles Revue, Coffee Butler, Johnny-Johnny, Popcorn Joe, Liz O'Connor**, and **Al Subarsky** in Key West.

Marilyn Kellner in the rock's Poet's Corner.

Patti Bright writing under the stairs.

JVM Rubin in Vienna.

And my intuitive, patient-as-a-saint editor **GL Rotocampo** in the UK.

TABLE OF INCONTINENCE

37—The Spice Girls
38—Nick Carter
39—Bob Marley
40—Jim Croce
41—Kenny Chesney
42—Jerry Jeff Walker
43—Frank Gifford and Curt Gowdy
44—The Beach Boys
45—Michael McDonald
46—The Tennessee Williams Theatre
47—George Strait
48—Major Orestes Lorenzo Perez
49—The Blue Paper
50—The Revivalists
51—David Wolkowsky
52—Richard Burton
53—James Leo Herlihy
54—James Kirkwood
55—Robert Frost
56—Jessie Porter
57—Ernest Hemingway
58—Martha Gellhorn
59—Jackie Gleason
60—Jimmy Buffett
61—Rudolf Nureyev
62—Joe Cocker
63—*True Lies*, the movie
64—David Robinson
65—Sam Hochman
66—JFK
67—Fidel Castro
68—Colin Powell
69—Boog Powell
70—Thomas Edison
71—Mel Fisher
72—John James Audubon
73—Goldie Hawn
74—Stephen Fetchit

75—Kelly McGillis
76—Diana Nyad
77—Bill Clinton
78—Oprah
79—Michael Keaton
80—Madonna
81—Daisy Fuentes
82—Robert Redford
83—Henry Flagler
84—Charles Lindbergh
85—Juan Terry Trippe
86—Capt. Tony
87—Mayor Gonzo Mays
88—Freddy Cabanas
89—Will Soto
90—Jenna Stauffer
91—Al Subarsky
92—The Key West Island Bookstore
93—Harry Teaford
94—Cindy Williams
95—Penny Leto
96—Duane "Bongo D" Scott
97—David L. Sloan
98—Sallie Foster
99—Nick Norman
100—The Cookie Lady
101—Gary Hempsey
102—Popcorn Joe
103—Fats Navarro
104—Coffee Butler
105—Cliff Sawyer
106—Barry Cuda
107—Tom Luna
108—Caffeine Carl
109—Robert Albury
110—Harry Powell
111—Randy Roberts
112—Sushi

CELEBRITIES PAST AND PRESENT

Okay, here we go at last, a cheeky tribute to the righteous giants and geniuses who helped shaped our island, and those who continue to do so to this day.

This list is NOT exhaustive, so apologies if I failed to include one of your favorites, that plus many folk of suspect background, questionable mental health and/or sobriety have begged me not to give them a mention until they're out on work-release.

CHAPTER 1—Bum Farto

Joseph "Bum" Farto was the Fire Chief of Key West from 1964 until 1975.

He was a good guy. Supremely competent. Highly respected. And wildly popular.

He was also a serial adulterer, a practitioner of Santeria, and a drug dealer.

Folk tend to forget all the good you've done for the community when you're busted for selling weed and blow from a sunny bench in front of your very own fire station.

Cursed with a lamentable familial appellation, Farto was born in Key West the day before the Fourth of July in the year 1919 (did this portend future endeavors?).

He was the son of Juan Farto, a Spanish immigrant who owned and operated the Victoria Restaurant at the corner of Greene and Duval, address 201 Duval.

AUTHOR'S GIN-JOINT NOTE: Did you recognize the address? Well done you! Indeed, the one-and-only same location of present day Sloppy Joe's.

Little Farto grew up in a wood-frame house right behind the Victoria Restaurant and just around the corner from the old red-brick fire station behind City Hall. This was the home of Hook & Ladder No. 1.

Farto idolized the firemen and hung out there after school. He asked a lot of questions, and begged constantly for spare change (even as a boy, he liked the cash and he liked buying things). The firemen thought Farto was a gas, took a liking to him, made him a mascot of sorts, and presented him with the endearing moniker "Bum."

As a teenager, Bum first worked at his father's restaurant

where they served the "best yellowtail in Cayo Hueso" but flogging yellowtail was not his calling. Then he did a few years in the embalming room at the Lopez Funeral Home (now the Dean-Lopez Funeral Home) at 418 Simonton, but the presence of corpses and the waft of formaldehyde just did not float his boat ether, I mean either.

He had a burning desire to be a fireman, and a fireman he became.

At the age of 19, Farto joined the Key West Fire department.

By the age of 22, Bum had become a nozzleman (you get to hold your own hose).

Eventually he made captain.

Then, by the age of 45, he was named chief.

**A SPORTY NOTE: Bum Farto loved baseball, Key West High School baseball to be exact. As Fire Chief, he used to drive his lime-green Cadillac convertible with the white sidewalls and gold spread-eagle hood ornament, and the personalized vanity front plate, which read: "El Jefe," right into the baseball stadium, park it over behind the fence in left field and, being a devotee of Santeria, he would root his home team on by lighting a black ritual candle, placing it on the fender of his beloved Eldorado and casting a spell.

That's loyalty!

BTW: *Placing a curse* does NOT fall in the same league of fandom as rallying a crowd by waving a Steelers black-and-gold Terrible Towel, bellowing the Vikings Nordic Skol chant, or cheering on the Milwaukee Brewers Racing Sausages.

Some said Farto was a flamboyant eccentric, a flashy dresser with his fire-engine red, or all-white John Travolta/*Saturday Night Fever* disco suits, dripping in gold chains and flashing the bling with gold rings and bracelets and watches, and even rose-tinted sunglasses.

Others would simply say he had really bad taste.

Perhaps Farto had not been spending enough time in the cool shade, thus the selling of drugs out of the fire station, or out of his official KWFD wheels.

But, then again, Key West was different back then:

--Fishing boats brazenly unloaded bales of marijuana on local docks.

--High school students in the hunt for a part-time job were paid big bucks to borrow the car from daddy and drive the Chevy past the levee loaded with bales of weed up the Overseas Highway to Little Havana. (It was not known if they received extra credit for the few phrases of street Spanish learned during transactions. *¡Hola, puta! ¿Qué cojones estás haciendo aquí?*)

--Drug dealers partied long and hard, tooting up right in many Duval Street watering holes.

--Upstanding homeowners were offered upwards of $20,000 if they would rent the dock in front of their waterfront homes for the weekend and turn a blind eye so a bit of unloading and passage through the backyard to a waiting truck parked out front could take place.

--Middle-of-the-night, speeding cigarettes, Zodiacs and Rivas could be heard running, lights off, close to shore.

--Even the echoing report of distant sporadic gunfire was audible.

Farto may have been a misguided, albeit greedy, entrepreneur, but he wasn't alone. Bolita sellers roamed Duval, Whitehead and Petronia, chanting: "Last call for the numbers!" and that had nothing to do with the Cuban lottery.

Square groupers were the Catch o' Day.

T-shirts for sale in Duval Street shop windows proclaimed "SMOKE FLORIDA SEAFOOD."

And cocaine was as common as Key lime pie.

Many folk back then didn't really give a slippery rat's ass how you made ends meet as locals had fallen on hard times when the Navy, which had been a cash cow for local businesses since 1823, pulled a good chunk of its presence out of Key West.

In 1971, President Nixon declared war on drugs, by significantly increasing the size and presence of federal drug control agencies, and pushing through measures such as mandatory sentencing and "no-knock" warrants.

In 1973, the DEA was formed, creating another anti-drug-smuggling-and-distribution weapon in the arsenal.

The writing was on the wall—in blood—but Bum Farto was too busy dealing to read the fine print.

Mind you, Farto wasn't a druggie. He didn't sell drugs to get high or blow out his septum, he sold drugs to enrich his flamboyant image and build lavish extensions on his house on United Street (and just around the corner from Tennessee Williams).

Drug trafficking through Key West became too much for then Governor Reubin Askew to bear and he was feeling the heat, so he enlisted the help of some friends in the Broward County State Attorney's Office. That department's findings were enough to begin a six-month investigation led by the DEA, the Florida Department of Criminal Law Enforcement and the Dade County Organized Crime Bureau.

And "Operation Conch" was born.

Enter an ex-junkie-turned-informant by the name of Titus Walters. Titus introduced a "cousin" of his to Farto to score some coke, problem was the "cousin" wasn't really a cousin, rather an undercover narcotics officer. You can see how this was going to play out, can't you?

Bad for Bum, worse for Titus, as someone snitched and Titus ended up abducted, injected with Drano, then injected with battery acid. When that didn't kill him, presumably because all the smack he had shot up in his life had been cut with even more vile shit, the hitman stuffed Titus in a bathtub and then shot him twice in the head. This should have been enough of an effort for most, but Titus Walters just wasn't ready to take leave of this earth, so his kidnapper jammed his pistol deep in to Titus' chest and shot him once more, this time straight through the heart.

Fearing the possibility of leaks, the Operation Conk task force purposely kept the local sheriff, police chief and city attorney in the dark about a pending raid.

In September of 1975, twenty eight agents dressed like the Men in Black (wearing ties in the Key West heat: this should have raised warning flags) descended on the island and checked into the Key Wester Motel posing as karate enthusiasts (as one

11

does), and subsequently launched the first "Bubba Bust," rounding up all low-life drug dealers, including said city attorney (who just happened to be the police chief's son), a bail bondsman, and none other than the Fire Chief of Key West, Joseph "Bum" Farto himself.

**AUTHOR'S SHIT ON A SHINGLE NOTE: These Bubba Busts occurred in 1975, 1985 and again in 1995. Those caught in the tangled web that Cayo Hueso itself had weaved included: a Key West mayor, a city commissioner, a city attorney, said fire chief, a deputy police chief, all that plus an opened can of worms in the squiggly form of guv'mint employees, lots of other cops, local mobsters and, are you ready, a school bus driver who was caught selling drugs out of his big yellow school bus. (The wheels on a bus may go round and round, but so do the wheels of Justice)

Joseph's "Bum" Farto's trial was set for February.

At the trial, the jury didn't need long to deliberate. Either the evidence was overwhelming or they had someplace else to be because they only hung around for just over a half an hour. Farto's life was about to go pear-shaped. He was convicted on one count of selling marijuana and two counts of selling cocaine. The honorable judge set sentencing for April. For his transgressions, he faced thirty-one years in the BIG HOUSE instead of the FIRE HOUSE.

Bum Farto was about to get hosed.

Three days later, Bum Farto, free on $25,000 bond, told his long-suffering wife, Esther, he had to go up to the mainland to hook up with a friend. ("Gee, honey-buns, I'm about to go spend the rest of my life in the slammer. I got nothing going today, so I think I'll just drive the 130 miles up around Miami International Airport to meet a friend for a *con leche*. I'll pick up a half dozen *empanadas*. I'll be home before dark. Sure I will."

Farto took nothing with him, not even votive candles.

He had wanted to motor on up the Overseas Highway in his fire department official car—a *lime-green* Ford LTD—but that had been confiscated on the grounds that it had been used to transport drugs. Then, get ready for this, the tow truck that was supposed to be used to tow away Farto's LTD had to be impounded, as well, because it too had been used to transport drugs.

Bum Farto ended up having to rent a *red* Pontiac LeMans from Hargis Chevron on Truman Avenue, which he did, then he sped north as fast as fast can go.

Three weeks elapsed before a light dimly flickered in Mrs. Farto's brain and she called the Monroe County Sheriff's Office. She told the sheriff that she had not seen her dear Bum since the day he left to drive to Miami.

"Didn't it cross your mind that something might be amiss? Didn't you think it would have been prudent to call us about two weeks and six days earlier?"

Was she covering for Bum, or was she just one beer short of a six-pack? Perhaps life had been nice and quiet around the ol' homestead on United, and she wasn't about to muck with the formula?

Police scrambled and searched parking lots at Miami International Airport, but they found no trace of the red Pontiac LeMans that Farto had rented.

Meanwhile, Hargis Chevron filed a stolen-car complaint against Farto. The car, a company spokesman said, had been due back the day it was rented. Duhhh.

Finally, on March 22, the red LeMans was found parked on Calle Ocho, near the historic heart of Miami's vibrant Little Havana.

Did Bum Farto fall afoul of the Tampa or Miami mafia?

Or Columbian cocaine cowboys?

Was he flown in a private aircraft over the Everglades and then unceremoniously told to take a leap of faith out into the wild blue yonder?

Or did he end up living the good life down in Costa Rica as was rumored, with a new 16-year-old *chica* supplied each year by gangster friends?

Somebody knows, but no one is talking.

I wonder if anyone had checked to see if he had taken his passport when he rode out of town?

Have a cheeky CLICK on this link when you get the urge.

It's circa 1930, and shows St. Joseph's School in Key West, FL. Little Bum Farto is in the front row, holding the school pennant, fifth from the left.

https://www.flickr.com/photos/97623182@N00/28899679392

**AUTHOR'S OMG NOTE: In 1881, the Sisters of Holy Names of Jesus and Mary established St. Joseph's School. "Dedicated to the education of *white* boys."

CHAPTER 2—The Queen of England

The Queen (yes, the real one) and that rascal of a husband of hers, Prince Phillip, visited the Dry Tortugas (a small group of islands 70 miles west of Key West) in May of 1991. The esteemed and first woman mayor of Monroe County, Wilhelmina Harvey, was on hand to greet the Queen and present her with a beautiful pink and white conch shell (a *queen* conch shell) and an Honorary Conch certificate.

The Queen and Prince Phillip had sailed down from Miami on the 412-foot *Royal Yacht Britannia* and had anchored just off historic Fort Jefferson, one of the nation's largest 19th century forts.

On account of the Queen being present onboard, the Royal Yacht had been escorted by a Royal Navy warship, riding shotgun…in the hot sun.

Also onboard the Royal Yacht itself for security measures was a platoon of Royal Marines.

The Queen wanted to see the fort and especially the cell where the American physician Samuel Mudd had been imprisoned for purportedly conspiring with John Wilkes Booth to assassinate U.S. President Abraham Lincoln in 1865, so she jumped in a tender and stormed the fort.

I remember this being a pretty big deal back then.

Wilhelmina Harvey was "Admiral and First Sea Lord of the Conch Republic Navy". So pretty much royalty herself.

**MY BAD NOTE: Perhaps the Queen of England didn't know…or perhaps she didn't give a flying royal…what with her being, well, the Queen, but conch shells or fragments of said conch shells brought into the UK are NOT allowed entry as conch shells are on the list of banned items.

In the UK, conch shells are the 9th-most seized import.

The Queen's name was Mud.

CHAPTER 3—Dr. Hunter S. Thompson

Are you sitting down?

Strong drink in hand?

Dog at your feet?

Cat on your lap?

Dog wondering why he can't be up on your lap instead of the cat?

To give you a bit of insight into what sort of journalist that enigmatic scunner Dr. Hunter S. Thompson was: When he would leave home and go off on assignment, which was frequent, he would take along the required items he felt he needed to survive the journey and the hotel stay, be it protracted or short-lived. If it was you or me going on a road trip, we might take along some Salt & Vinegar Pringles (or perhaps Prawn Cocktail, perhaps not), a couple 16oz jars of Planters Dry Roasted Peanuts (slightly salted), extra contact lenses (+2.75 both right and left), a few packs of Wrigley's or Extra chewing gum, a length of dental floss (or dental tape), Tums (on account of the Pringles), a cheeky flask of Southern Comfort or Jim Beam, perhaps even a dash/splash/vial/small plastic bag of guilty pleasure, a Snickers, nibbles for the dog, one condom in case you get lucky…one paper bag in case you're unlucky.

But this is what made Hunter S. Thompson different from you and me. He wrote about this as it was indeed oft his modus operandi: "The trunk of the car looked like a mobile police narcotics lab. We had two bags of grass, seventy-five pellets of mescaline, five sheets of high-powered blotter acid, a salt shaker half full of cocaine, and a whole galaxy of multi-colored uppers, downers, screamers, laughers and also a quart of tequila, a quart of rum, a case of Budweiser, a pint of raw ether and two dozen amyls…

"…Not that we needed all that for the trip, but once you

16

get locked into a serious drug collection, the tendency is to push it as far as you can. The only thing that really worried me was the ether. There is nothing in the world more helpless and irresponsible and depraved than a man in the depths of an ether binge. And I knew we'd get into that rotten stuff pretty soon."

WTF!

Hunter Thompson spent nearly two years living, riding, drinking, druggin', and shooting off firearms with the Hell's Angels so that he could more accurately pen a book about the outlaw motorcycle gang and "take readers deep inside a subculture largely inaccessible to the outside world."

That's taking research to the next level.

**FY-bleary eye for the drunk guy-I: I'll sit my ass on a barstool at The Bull to deliver accurate reportage, but I'm not about to ride with the outlaws. But, then again, there are a fair few outlaws in The Bull anyway, aren't there?

Hunter Thompson's book *Hell's Angels* was a critical and financial success. So much so, the Hell's Angels felt they were being exploited and they wanted a piece of the royalties' pie.

But Hunter arrogantly and greedily refused.

So the Hell's Angels said: "Well, okay." Then they beat the livin' shit out of him.

Hunter Stockton Thompson was born in Louisville, Kentucky on 18 July 1937 (What is it about July babies?).

Thompson has been described thusly by various sources, many of them sober and clean:

"Gonzo journalist."

"Charismatic magnet."

"Beacon for dissent."

"Ether huffer."

"Drug-fueled narcissist."

"Professional fall-down drunk."

"Speed freak."

"Button-pushing, old-fashioned anarchist."

"A lover of guns and books from right out of the womb."

"Southern gentleman."

"And the greatest American comic writer of the 20th

century." (This opined by famed author Tom Wolfe.)

Hunter Thompson was the counter-culture author of *Fear and Loathing in Las Vegas*, and his close friend Johnny Depp starred as a "Hunter-esque" character in the eponymous movie adaptation, a road film, which was released in 1998 and distributed by Universal Pictures.

Hunter was also an off-and-on resident in Key West, vacillating between the rock and the Rockies (Aspen).

Okay, let me show you something. Jump on you bicycle and let's pedal over to the other side of the island to Louie's Backyard.

Okay, I'm here now.

Is that you?

Have you been waiting long? You beat me here. I started at our sailboat in the Bight and I stopped for a shot of espresso at the Key Lime Pie Bakery on Greene. Needed the rocket fuel.

Where did you start from?

Well done! You made good time.

Okay, we're straddling our bikes in front of Louie's Backyard Restaurant. To the right, you can see Dog Beach. See the woman with the pug? She lives on Stock Island. She brings her fur-baby here for a special day out.

Now look to the left. See that house? It's right on the water. Hunter Thompson lived in the apartment right up there. It was loaned to him by Jimmy Buffett.

They were buds.

The good doctor would sleep late, sometimes till noon, sometimes till four in the afternoon, and sometimes he would simply stay up all night long.

When he did sleep, he would rise like a brown bear exhuming itself from hibernation, call out for a pizza, pour himself an adult beverage, light up a fag, snort a line or pop an upper, and get down to the serious business of writing some snappy crackling prose.

Or perhaps just making a helluva lot of copious notes.

His mind was always on fire.

Not surprising, what with the consumption of a boat-load of Schedule 2 drugs (Class A drugs in the UK).

Alas, when darkness settled in, the beast in him would emerge once again and, surrounded by a gaggle of coke whores, he would spend the evenings and the wee hours metamorphosing into Bacchus the god of partying, commuting between the Green Parrot and the Chart Room at the Pier House, drinking and smoking and tooting and holding sway.

He just had to be the center of attention.

One night Hunter took his fall-down-drunkenness to a new level. You see, he kept a small speedboat down here and this one night, about midnight, he was so fucked up, he fell out of his boat as he was trying to dock it.

As Hunter swam ashore to save his soaked sorry-ass, he looked back to see his boat doing concentric doughnuts, crashing into other boats as it wreaked absolute mayhem in the marina.

There's a tribute of sorts to this late-night dockage fiasco over at the Green Parrot, so you might want to pop over there later and see it for yourself.

On occasion, after wearing out his welcome in Key West's Old Town, Thompson would peregrinate fifteen-plus miles up the Overseas Highway to Sugarloaf Key, taking his wrecking ball of his latest girlfriend and baying coke hounds to annex the Sugarloaf Lodge, one of his coveted tranquil idylls.

Perhaps not so tranquil for the other paying guests in the neighboring rooms as he would party, fight and fornicate noisily all night long.

Always with an eye on expansion and reinvention—this would be the mid-70s—Thompson paid for an Ad in the local Yellow Pages. "High-speed, no running lights, midnight tours of the Florida Keys. See the soft underbelly of the Florida Keys."

**AUTHOR'S DISCONCERTING NOTE: When I lived in Aspen in the 70s, I used to walk past a Head Shop in the center of the glitzy ski resort where Hunter Thompson's wife worked. You could see her in there, beavering away, smiling a lot, as she sold a bong, some papers, baby laxative or a screen.

I guess it's correct to assume that Hunter got a family discount.

There was a posh restaurant in Aspen back then called the Arya and it was located at the foot of Aspen Mountain, pretty much in the center of town. The place was expensive, and they had one large dining room called the "American Room." And they had four or five private dining rooms, much smaller, perhaps able to seat 8-10 diners. The private rooms didn't have doors, but they had curtains…and EVERYTHING went on in there behind the drapes.

I know this because I was the maître d'.

I'd landed the job because I was the caretaker of a millionaire couple's manse up on Red Mountain, just on the other side of the narrow valley, and the couple owned the restaurant. Their neighbor was bestselling-author Leon Uris and his then wife Jill. Leon and Jill would be over for lunch and there I was polishing the silver or running the dishwasher.

This book is about Key West, so I don't want to prattle on about Aspen, but the two communities have always been bound at the hip (or the septum).

And, yes, Hunter Thompson patronized the Arya, not often, but when he did, I had to close the place up and lock the doors. I spent more than a few nights, dressed in my fancy-smancy tuxedo and my patent-leather shoes, in front of the fireplace waiting for Hunter and his posse to run out of coke so they would leave and I could go home.

Then, one radiantly memorable night at the Woody Creek Tavern near Aspen, there was much to do about everything as shots rang out on the backside of midnight, but it was just Hunter firing his pistol in the air announcing his arrival as he pulled up in his Jeep.

Scared the living shit out of all present.

At least he hadn't brought the cattle prod when he used to patronize the Arya. More on that electrifying late-night interlude below.

* * *

Here for your scrotum-shriveling entertainment, a few defining Hunter S. Thompson quotes:

"I drink alcohol like I smoke cigarettes; I don't even notice

20

it. You know, a bird flies, a fish swims, I drink."

"A cap of good acid cost $5 and for that you can hear the Universal Symphony with God singing solo and the Holy Ghost on drums."

"I hate to advocate drugs, alcohol, violence, or insanity to anyone, but they've always worked for me."

AUTHOR'S SOTTO VOCE NOTE: With Hunter Thompson, you never knew if he was going to implode or explode.

Hunter S. Thompson's personal mazes had monsters. His demons even had their own demons. After leaving Key West and returning to the Rockies, he committed suicide at the age of 67 on his 42-acre Owl Farm, just down river from Aspen. He sat down in his favorite chair in his kitchen, stuffed the barrel of one of his beloved .45-caliber pistols in his mouth and blew his brains out all over the back wall.

His grown son and grandkid were in the house. It takes a mushy mind or the height of narcissism to blow your brains out with kids in the house.

In accordance with his wishes, his ashes were FIRED OUT OF A CANNON as red, white, blue and green fireworks lit up the night, and "Spirit in the Sky" blared loudly from enormous speakers over the grieving, hooting, rowdy assembled. The private ceremony was financed by Johnny Depp to the eye-watering tune of $3 million. "All I'm doing is trying to make sure his last wish comes true," Depp was quoted. "I just want to send my pal out the way he wants to go out."

In attendance were 280 friends and souls of similar ilk, or not, including John Kerry, George McGovern, Sean Penn, John Cusack, Jack Nicholson, Bill Murray, Josh Hartnett, Lyle Lovett, and a few close friends from Key West.

The cannon which fired the ashes had been positioned atop a 153-foot tower which had the shape of a double-thumbed fist clutching a peyote button. This image was the same symbol Thompson used when he unsuccessfully ran for Sheriff of Pitkin County (Aspen is the county seat).

A touching funeral and appropriate send-off, though

arguably not as intimate as having your ashes snorted off the bar at the Chart Room at the Pier House in Key West as a few despondent locals have done with their deceased one's remains. I will soon address that expression of grief, but until then…

CHECK OUT these two YouTube videos. Ensure you are sitting down:

#1 Hunter's funeral:
https://www.youtube.com/watch?v=v9ReDDDC0Rg

#2 Johnny Depp talking about Hunter on David Letterman:
https://www.youtube.com/watch?v=zkWupnH8Uvs

And where did the "Dr." come from in Dr. Hunter S. Thompson?
He made it up.

CHAPTER 4—Gene Hackman

An occasional visitor to Key West, he was spotted in Marathon buying a doggie door at a pet store not too long ago. I find this adorably commendable. When many other celebrities go out of their way to be rude, stand-offish and effing snobs, our man Gene Hackman throws on a pair of shorts and flip-flops, and goes out and buys a doggie door for his pooch.

How can you not like someone who does that?

Pretty remarkable for a fellow who has won two Oscars and been nominated three other times. Having said that, Gene Hackman's dog doesn't know about the Oscars or the nominations and thinks Gene is pretty cool anyway, what with the purchase of the aforementioned doggie door.

CHAPTER 5—Louis Armstrong

Louis Daniel Armstrong was born in the impoverished, gang-drug-and-prostitute infested Battlefield section of New Orleans on August 4, 1901. His mother was sixteen, and the birth took place at home. Soon after his birth, Armstrong's father took off and Armstrong was raised by his grandmother until he was five, then his mother re-entered the picture and took up her maternal responsibilities.

The Battlefield section of New Orleans was called "Darktown" by the white Press.

Satchmo preferred to call it "Soulville."

AUTHOR'S BOOZY NOTE: Let me digress from Louis Armstrong for a moment and set the stage with the following: During the years of Prohibition (1920 to 1933), the Southernmost House, at the corner of Duval and South, in Key West, operated as a "speakeasy," rum-running whisky and rum from Cuba. **Josie Russell** was one of those rum-runners.

The first floor of the Southernmost House functioned as a restaurant. The next floor up was a small casino. On the third floor nothing was taboo.

During Prohibition, the Southernmost House catered to celebrities and gangsters, and really anyone who was well-heeled, those who were on their way to Havana stopped off to spend a few nights and spend some money before taking the ferry or, starting in 1928, Pan Am across the Florida Straits to Havana.

ANOTHER BOOZY NOTE: When Prohibition came, American bartenders fled America in the droves—for Cuba. It was reported that a dozen out-of-work bartenders quit Chicago for Havana—daily.

Havana of the 1920s had over 7,000 bars and virtually every one of them had American bartenders.

In the 1940s, the Southernmost House was used as a nightclub called "Café Cayo Hueso." Many of the usual suspects frequented the venue: Hemingway (after he'd dumped Pauline), Tennessee Williams, Truman Capote, a young Gore Vidal, Tallulah Bankhead (during the filming of *Lifeboat* in 1944), Gloria Swanson ("Alright, Mr. DeMille, I'm ready for my close-up"), Charles Lindbergh…and, yes, Louis Armstrong.

In the 1950s, Armstrong would return to Key West and play at a venue that is now where the Coral City Elks Club is located near the corner of Whitehead and Amelia. Walk on over there, it's near "Anchors Aweigh."

Armstrong died of a heart attack in his sleep on July 6, 1971, in Queens, NYC, a month before his 70th birthday. At his funeral it was patently obvious how much-loved and well-respected this man was. His honorary pallbearers included Dizzy Gillespie, Pearl Bailey, Count Basie, Harry James, Bing Crosby, Ella Fitzgerald, Earl Wilson, Alan King, David Frost, Ed Sullivan, Johnny Carson, and Frank Sinatra.

Peggy Lee sang "The Lord's Prayer."

Al Hibbler sang "Nobody Knows the Trouble I've Seen."

You may know that the airport in New Orleans was named after Armstrong in 2001: "Louis Armstrong New Orleans International Airport."

The New Orleans airport purports to be the "second lowest-lying international airport in the world at 4-feet feet above sea level."

In fact, Key West International Airport is the true second-lowest in the world, coming in at 3-feet above sea level.

What's the lowest-lying international airport in the world you ask?

That would be Amsterdam's Schiphol International, which is…are you ready?…11-feet *below* sea level.

CHAPTER 6—Gloria Swanson

Hollywood starlet, Gloria Swanson was petite, measuring in at a diminutive 4-feet-eleven inches, but height didn't matter on the big screen when you had that sort of magnetism, and she became our "silent movie queen."

Her father was a civilian supply officer in the Army. The family moved frequently and she grew up in Chicago, Puerto Rico, and Key West.

Swanson cherished her years in Key West and got a big kick out of living on the Army base.

As an adult, she frequently returned to spend time on the rock or use it as a stopover on her way to Cuba.

She was fluent in Spanish.

In 1929, Swanson was nominated for the *first* Academy Award for Best Actress.

Gloria Swanson has two stars on the Hollywood Walk of Fame—one for motion pictures located at 6748 Hollywood Blvd., and one for television at 6301 Hollywood Blvd.

Immortalized in Hollywood.

Beloved in Key West.

CHAPTER 7—Alfred Hitchcock

Hitchcock said these "fighting words" while visiting Zadar, Croatia, in May of 1964: "Zadar has the most beautiful sunset in the world, more beautiful than the one in Key West in Florida, applauded at every evening."

**AUTHOR'S DISGRUNTLED NOTE: I beg to differ. The sun in Zadar generally sets behind distant mountains and you will never see the sun squat on the horizon or catch a glimpse of the elusive green flash. At least our sun moves to the left or the right of Sunset Key, allowing for that opportunity, the squatting and the flashing of green.

CHAPTER 8—Shel Silverstein

Sheldon Allan Silverstein turned up in Key West in the late 60s and rented second-floor digs in a conch house on the corner of Caroline and Ann (525 Caroline, to be exact). Silverstein's "landlady" was a colorful, full-time character and part-time whacko, so that begs two questions:

Was she the cheeky vixen immortalized in Jimmy Buffett's song, "Woman Gone Crazy on Caroline Street"?

Was in fact *she* really a *he*? A transvestite?

> **"There's a woman goin' crazy on Caroline Street.**
> **Stoppin' every man that she does meet**
> **Sayin' if you'll be gentle if you'll be sweet**
> **I'll show you my place on Caroline Street."**

Then, in the 1980s, Silverstein purchased a wooden—made partially of Dade County pine—two-story 1901 Greek Revival house with adjacent writer's studio at 618 William Street for forty-three thousand dollars (In 2017, and prior to Hurricane Irma, it was worth well over 1.3 million).

Two majestically expansive and towering banyan trees held sway in front of the house and provided much needed shade in the summer, most of the year, actually.

Silverstein loved to sing and he could be found on occasion gigging at the Hog's Breath or Capt. Tony's.

Next time you're in Capt. Tony's, look for the 1982 photo of Shel and Capt. Tony.

And Silverstein was much the ladies' man and he had a temporal union with a woman who drove the Conch Tour Train. This tryst produced Shel's song "The Great Conch Train Robbery," and a son named Matt, born out of wedlock.

When Gabrielle and I lived downstairs at Sam Hochman's at 704 Caroline, we'd have our front door propped open in a failed attempt to beckon in a breath of fresh, non-humid air. We'd see Shel Silverstein come up the steps onto the porch and then enter Sam's and slip upstairs to smoke some "green and gold and glorious," and plan their next trip to Bangkok.

Our landlord Sam would get pretty ripped late, and become quite loquacious and tell us about those trips to Bangkok with Shel and all the women they had and all the kinky things that the sensual Thai girls would show them that could be done with beads and knotted silk rope.

It was an eye-opener.

FLASHBACK: Around about 1956, Hugh Hefner was getting a new magazine up and running called, yes, *Playboy*, and Hefner was a frustrated cartoonist. He gave Shel a job creating naughty cartoons and eventually a travelogue. This afforded Silverstein enough dosh to give up his day job: selling hotdogs at Wrigley Field and Comiskey Park.

Silverstein was prolific, having written over 800 songs and more than 100 one-act plays. His children's books have been translated into thirty-plus languages, and have sold over 20 million copies, and continue to kick ass on the best-sellers lists.

He wrote the song "I'm Checking Out," for the 1990 Oscar nominated film *Postcards from the Edge*. It was nominated for an Oscar for Best Original Song. The movie was directed by Mike Nichols, screenplay by Carrie Fisher, and had an illustrious cast: Meryl Streep, Shirley MacLaine, Dennis Quaid, Gene Hackman, Richard Dreyfuss, Annette Bening, Rob Reiner, and Gary Morton.

He won a Grammy for the song "A Boy Named Sue," sung by Johnny Cash and recorded live at San Quentin. Have you ever listened to the response of the inmates? They absolutely embraced the song's lyrics and loved Johnny Cash.

No surprise there.

"Well, my daddy left home when I was three
And he didn't leave much to ma and me
Just this ole guitar and an empty bottle of booze
Now I don't blame him 'cause he run and hid
But the meanest thing that he ever did
Was before he left he went and named me Sue…"

A boy named Sue and as you will now see "a tree named banyan."

**MILDLY INTERESTING BOTANICAL NOTE: A banyan tree starts life as an air plant, drops its seeds on a "host" (palm tree, pole, or a building) and aerial roots descend to take root in the soil, "strangling" its host along the way. Thus, the common term "strangler fig." Did you know this? I didn't.

Curiously, over the years, the banyan tree out front of Shel's house, and its aerial root system, engulfed a bicycle and slowly lifted it off the ground leaving it mid-tree and securely entombed. Until recently, it could be spotted if you opened the front gate and eyeballed it from that vantage point.

"Once there was a tree," Silverstein wrote in his *The Giving Tree*, a 1964 bestseller. Did you ever read that?

Once there was a tree, indeed. That bitch Hurricane Irma toppled both majestic banyan trees crushing the structure that once had been Silverstein's house. The beloved, albeit now offending banyan trees have been hoisted back into place and temporarily supported. Hope springs eternal that they will re-root, anchor and continue to flourish. Perhaps asking a lot for towering trees well over 200-hundred years old which had originally taken root in the shallow veneer of existing topsoil resting upon the island's rock-hard marl.

**AUTHOR'S-I-do-give-a-fig-NOTE: The largest Banyan Tree in the world is in India, in the state of Andhra Pradesh. It spans an eyes-growing-stalks 4.7 acres and can provided shade for up to—are you ready?— 20,000 people! Think about that the next time you are tooling around Key West on your bicycle, gazing with childlike wonder upon the glory that is Key West's very own banyan trees at locales such as: Porter Place, the post office, or the 300 block of Whitehead.

In 1999, two cleaning ladies entered Silverstein's house and verbally heralded their arrival. There was no answer.

They called out again.

Still no answer.

They discovered Uncle Shelby sitting up in bed—dead. He'd died of a massive heart attack some time between the evening of May 9 and the morning of May 10, cartooning and writing.

"Die doing what you love"—**Shel Silverstein**

CHAPTER 9—Ed Bradley

Yes, *that* Ed Bradley. We remember him best from CBS News *60 Minutes* (26-years' worth to be exact).

Bradley covered the fall of Saigon, was a White House correspondent, and many of us would tune in when he anchored his own news broadcast, *CBS Sunday Night News with Ed Bradley*.

When Ed Bradley wasn't sitting in front of a TV camera in New York City, he was chilling out in Aspen, Colorado, as an inveterate ski bum. He'd purchased a condo on Main Street after being introduced to the Rocky Mountain rural idyll by Hunter Thompson in 1976 when they were both keen reporters covering the campaign trails of future presidential hopefuls.

And he was *tight* with Hunter Thompson. So tight, in fact, he eventually sold his condo in the center of Aspen and purchased a house across the river from Hunter in Woody Creek, just downriver.

As Ed Bradley told it: "I moved to Woody Creek because of Hunter. He invited me in 1976 to come out to Aspen for a weekend. I fell in love with the valley and ended up buying a condominium in town. And then got tired of the bustle of town and bought a house on a quiet dead-end road in Woody Creek. Hunter and I were neighbors."

MAP NOTE: Bradley lived in an area of the Roaring Fork valley called Twinning Flats, just across the Roaring Fork River, from the aforementioned Woody Creek.

As you now know, Hunter Thompson loved being the center of attention and he loved doing the unexpected. Once, while Ed Bradley was playing a round of golf at the Aspen Municipal Golf Course, Hunter snuck up behind him and fired off a shotgun to distract the "60 Minutes" newsman in mid-swing.

Bradley was amused.

Thompson was arrested.

On another occasion, Hunter Thompson told Bradley: "There's someone I would like you to meet!" Then he flew Bradley over 2000 miles south to Key West and introduced him to—yes, you've got it—Jimmy Buffett.

Buffet and Bradley immediately hit it off and became lifelong friends.

Jimmy Buffett said this about Ed Bradley: "I think what we had in common was our nomadic sense of being. And we were travelers, and we were kind of gypsies out there. He and his journalistic endeavors and me and music."

And for Bradley's predilection for liking a good time, Buffett said: "Everybody in my opinion needs a little Mardi Gras in their life, and he liked to have a little more than the average person on occasion."

When Ed Bradley married his Haitian-born fiancée of ten years (and 24 years his junior) at their home in Aspen, Jimmy Buffett provided the wedding music.

FAST FORWARD: Jimmy Buffett was performing at a concert in Hawaii when his wife called late one night and said: "You need to get back here and see Ed."

Buffett flew straight away to New York and was at his dear friend's bedside when Bradley succumbed to complications from chronic lymphocytic leukemia at the age of 65.

They had been close friends for 30 years.

CHAPTER 10—Thomas McGuane

McGuane lived in Key West's leafy Old Town at 416 Elizabeth Street and 123-125 Ann Street, and at 1011 Von Phister.

Hard to hit a moving target.

McGuane is a best-selling author, manure-booted rancher, deep-sea fisherman…perhaps not in that order any more, as he's now content being a rancher up in Montana.

In the 70s, McGuane was anointed the "New Hemingway" by the Press. He was tall, a man's man, a sportsman, a fisherman, and possessed skirt-lifting charm and rugged good looks.

A chick-magnet.

A coke-whore magnet.

He was a graduate of Michigan State with a B.A. in English (where he met Jim Harrison), had an M.F.A. hanging on his wall from the Yale School of Drama, and was the recipient of the prestigious Wallace Stegner Fellowship from Stanford University.

**FYI: Wallace Stegner was an American novelist, short story writer, environmentalist, and historian, known among his peers as "The Dean of Western Writers." Stegner was awarded the Pulitzer Prize in 1972.

McGuane peregrinated back and forth from Livingston, Montana, to Key West, in the drug-fueled late 60s and 70s with his wife, Portia Rebecca Crockett, a direct descendent of none other than our "King of the Wild Frontier," Alamo-legend, gun-slinging hero Davy Crockett himself.

Writing novels during this period proved a tough way to make a living for young McGuane, so he turned to the more lucrative enterprise of writing screenplays for Hollywood. And here's what followed: He was known among his friends and hangers-on at party central as "Captain beserko" and wrote screenplays for the movie *Rancho Deluxe* (1973), shot in Livingston, Montana; *The Missouri Breaks* (1976), directed by Arthur Penn (Penn directed *Bonnie and Clyde*) and starring Jack Nicholson and Marlon Brando. Hollywood continued to call, so he called back and somehow sold them on producing a film from his much ballyhooed novel *Ninety-Two in the Shade*. And, through a combination of charm, intelligence and bravado, talked his way into directing it. No easy task for someone who had never directed anything other than the fastest way to get to the Chart Room from the Green Parrot. "Up to Duval, turn left, go until you hit the Gulf, listen for the guitar music…"

The novel *Ninety-Two in the Shade* became the film *92 in the Shade* (seemed to fit better on the marquee written that way), and it was shot on location in Key West, mostly at 336 Duval.

The movie starred Peter Fonda, Warren Oates, Margot Kidder, Elizabeth Ashley, Burgess Meredith, and Harry Dean Stanton.

Take notes now, as this next bit won't be easy to follow:

During filming, Tom McGaune's wife, Portia Rebecca Crockett, was sleeping with Warren Oates and then Peter Fonda.

Tom McGuane was sleeping with Elizabeth Ashley.

Tom McGuane dumped Elizabeth Ashley. She was not amused, so she hit him over the head with a lamp during filming.

Tom McGuane then began sleeping with the young starlet in *92 in the Shade*, Margot Kidder, that's Lois Lane to you and me.

Things were heating up, where's there's smoke there's fire, but nobody was calling Bum Farto.

After principal filming was completed and the beast was "in the can," Portia Rebecca Crockett divorced Tom McGuane. Crockett married Peter Fonda (they were hitched for 36 years).

Tom McGuane married Margot Kidder (she was from Yellowknife, Canada, and loved to fish, perhaps not enough though as the marriage only lasted six months. You could say she got skunked).

Tom McGuane divorced Margot Kidder.

Tom McGuane married the sister of one of his best friends. That friend was Jimmy Buffett, and Tom McGuane and Laurie

Buffett are still married.

**AUTHOR'S NOTE: I got a headache trying to write all that down and keep it straight and had to go lie down in a dark place. (And, no, it wasn't on the floor in the back corner of The Bull, although, perhaps, it should've been.)

CHAPTER 11—Peter Fonda

Fonda called Key West home from the mid-70s to the early 80s.

He used to live in Key West at, yes, 1011 Von Phister, in a house he purchased from friend—you got it—Tom McGuane.

Peter Fonda and Tennessee Williams were buds and used to hang together. Captain America was six-feet-two, Williams was five-feet-four on a good day. It was easy to see them coming.

Tennessee Williams used to roll opium-laced joints for Fonda.

Buds.

Easy Roller.

FLASH FORWARD: Round about 2015/2016, Peter Fonda hopped on his motorcycle up around Naples and rode down the state, into the Keys and onto the rock. And this is what he said about returning to Key West all these years later: "Boy, it was like I knew nothing about Key West. It has changed so much and it's like going into Las Vegas. I was totally disoriented. Nothing was the same."

Peter Fonda has just died as I write this, 16 August 2019: R.I.P. Captain America.

CHAPTER 12—Margot Kidder

Much like Lois Lane, Margot Kidder never minced her words, or bit her tongue, and she would tell anybody who listened that McGuane and Fonda and Jim Harrison (I will get to him soon), and the rest of their brat pack thought Key West in the early 70s was *their* Paris of the 1920s. She goes on: "Key West was a rather forced show that the guys put on for each other. It was all about Ernest Hemingway. It was just the Seventies' version of a jousting competition: who could take the most drugs and stay standing? They were all doing Ernest Hemingway, the 2nd—on coke…"

Kidder called it as she saw it.

And she was big on relationships.

Kidder dated former Canadian Prime Minister Pierre Trudeau, film director Brian De Palma, and writer/director Tom Mankiewicz. Even Steven Spielberg and comedian Richard Pryor.

She was married and divorced three times.

She was married to actor John Heard in 1979 for only six days, and was married to French film director Philippe de Broca from 1983 to 1984. After a messy divorce from de Broca, she said that she preferred the companionship of her dogs.

Understandable.

Kidder's first husband, Tom McGuane would tell you that "Kidder was the perfect choice to play the role of 'Miranda' in *92 in the Shade*, as she brought a pervasive sensuality to the role of the logical-minded schoolteacher and sex object of prospective fishing guide Tom Skelton, played by Peter Fonda."

As I've just mentioned above, although McGuane already had a wife (Portia Rebecca Crockett) and a sex-partner (Elizabeth Ashley) on the Key West set, he pursued Margot, and she offered little resistance.

"McGuane went for me because I *was* Miranda," Kidder said. "His first come-on line was, 'I bet you're one of those girls who writes *How true!* in the margins of your books.' It was the best line I've ever gotten. He had me hooked right then, because he was right."

Margot Kidder passed away at her home in Livingston, Montana, at the young age of 69.

* * *

ADDENDUM: Let me set this up by asking you a question or two: Ever feed the pigeons when you weren't supposed to? Put food out for the squirrels?

The seagulls?

The badgers?

Did you get told off by an angry neighbor or the town council. Get trashed on FB?

Well…this is what Margot Kidder did.

Writer, filmmaker, and consort of Margot Kidder, Ted Geoghegan revealed the following shortly after Kidder's death: "Margot loved the wolves that inhabited the mountains above her home just outside Livingston, Montana. Much to the chagrin of her neighbors and their pets, she left meat out for the wolves so she could watch them come down the mountain and eat from the safety of her home."

Ted went on to divulge: "She mentioned that she'd asked her closest friends—if they stopped by her place and found her dead—to tell no one, place her naked body in a bedsheet, drag it up Canyon Mountain, and leave her for her other friends, the wolves. If I had found the body, that's exactly what I would have done."

**UPDATE: On 9 August 2018, a coroner ruled Superman actress Margot Kidder's death was suicide.

Park County Coroner's office said she died "as a result of a self-inflicted drug and alcohol overdose."

A joint statement from the coroner's office and her family urged "those suffering from mental illnesses, addiction and/or suicidal thoughts to seek appropriate counselling and treatment."

CHAPTER 13—Elizabeth Ashley

Elizabeth Ashley was not only Tom McGuane's paramour *for a spell*, as you now know, she loved Key West and had a close and special friendship with Tennessee Williams.

"The reason I'm doing what I'm doing now is because of Tennessee Williams. The first play I ever saw and related to was *Summer and Smoke*. I must have been about 14, and I knew then I wanted to be an actress. Tennessee created a world I felt I knew."

She went on to say: "In order to negotiate life, most people sort of chart an emotional course to avoid the rocks and shoals, so your ship doesn't sink. But Tennessee wrote about all of those shoals and the monsters in the sea that come up and eat the boat. He went into the taboos of the heart and let us know that we don't have to carve out of our souls, the innocence and the madness … the things society wants to amputate. He saw life whole, not just the skin on the hand, but the bones and the blood in the veins beneath."

Tennessee Williams' death moved Elizabeth Ashley deeply, and she said: "They had to make his death lurid, didn't they? They just couldn't let it go by. Mongrels and curs always chew on the tail of champions, do they not? My mother always said, 'If you can't fly, go sit in the trees with the birds.' Well, a lot of people who can't fly feel it incumbent upon them to cut the wings off birds."

And: "Tenn was a gentleman, an aristocrat. And southern aristocrats were the best this country ever produced. Best of the breed. Hell, I was consigned to be a third-rate TV actress until I did *Cat on a Hot Tin Roof*."

And: "Maggie (the character she portrayed in *Cat on a Hot Tin Roof*) was a gift from him. But he also gave me sanity. The world has always been the emperor's new clothes to me.

Everybody talks about the suit of clothes and all I see is naked men. Tenn made me realize that the way I see the world is not a hallucination."

Elizabeth Ashley won a Tony Award for "Best Featured Actress in a Play" for *Take Her, She's Mine*, starred as Corie in the original Broadway production of Neil Simon's *Barefoot in the Park*, and played Maggie in a Broadway revival of *Cat on a Hot Tin Roof*.

She was nominated for a Tony for both performances.

BT-kinky-W: Elizabeth Ashley made her steamy romance with Tom McGuane in Key West (and further afield) radiantly public by documenting nearly every act of rip-roaring coitus in a tell-all memoir, with narrative such as "I'm into OD sex, excessive sex."

Lurid.

CHAPTER 14—Tom Brokaw

Where do you go to chill when you live and work in a city where everyone recognizes you and knows your every move?

You got it.

From time to time, Brokaw would slip away from the NBC anchor desk to come down to Key West to do some good ol' bonefish fishing with his pal Tom McGuane.

Brokaw has a ranch in Livingston, Montana, as well, and not far from Tom McGuane.

And Brokaw has always had a love/respect relationship with the flats around Key West: "What's so striking about the flats, so beautiful, the cumulus clouds, and full of green from the mangroves, yet they're so hostile. I mean, it really is a terrifying environment between the heat, no dry land to get to, no freshwater, and all the predators that are in the flats—barracuda, the sharks, everybody looking to eat everybody else…"

Key West flats fishing is like no other fishing in this great big world ours. Not saying it's better, just unique unto itself.

CHAPTER 15—Billy Crystal and Gregory Hines

"What the hell are we doing in Key West?" Billy Crystal asks.

And Gregory Hines replies. "It's as far south as we could get without having to speak Spanish."

This dialogue from their movie *Running Scared* which was filmed on location here.

Check out this movie clip to see what Key West was like in 1986 (and to see what it wasn't like, but jazzed up for the movie): https://www.youtube.com/watch?v=q3WJbJp0s-A

CHAPTER 16—The Beatles

I addressed this entry in short form in my last book **_KEY WEST: See It Before It Sinks_**. But here, oh joy, I give you the protracted version and with that a bit more background on what transpired down here that unforgettable night.

September, 1964, the Beatles multi-city United States and Canada tour takes off (the Beatles hit so many cities, the dates would've barely fit on the back of a T-shirt).

Manager Brian Epstein chartered a Lockheed Electra L-188 turboprop from American Flyers Airline for the tour.

The Fab Four had just gigged in Toronto and Montreal. Now they were headed to Jacksonville, Florida, to play in front of 32,000 screaming, swooning, delirious teenage girls and a smattering of boys at the Gator Bowl.

Tickets were pricey for 1964—$4 and $5.

Imagine.

And the tickets clearly stated "Rain or Shine."

Can you see where this is going?

The excitement and hoopla were off the charts.

But Mother Nature apparently wasn't into the Mersey Beat, and when the tickets had had "Rain or Shine" printed on them, no one was thinking about the Atlantic Hurricane Season.

Hurricane Dora began life off the coast of Senegal as a tropical wave, churned northeastward across the Atlantic and took aim at Florida's "First Coast," as a Category 4 menacing monster.

Just after midnight, on 10 September, Hurricane Dora made landfall as the eye passed over St. Augustine as a dangerous Category 3 storm.

Twenty-nine miles to the north, the brand-new Jacksonville Beach Pier was destroyed by punishing winds and freak storm surge.

Forty-three homes were lost out at the Jacksonville beaches—20 were swept right out to sea.

The Beatles were used to gales coming in off the Irish Sea back home in Liverpool, but they had never witnessed a tempest with this much fury.

Even in Blackpool.

ADD THIS TO THE MIX: Astonishingly, much of the South was still segregated in 1964, as was the case at the Gator Bowl. When the Beatles learned this, they balked and refused to play the Gator Bowl if the audience remained segregated. The promoters pushed mightily for desegregation and the Beatles won.

What's more, the Beatles were meant to stay in a hotel in Jacksonville, but when they heard that the hotel was segregated, as well, they balked again and said they would only stay if the hotel changed its policy.

The hotel refused.

So they said "Bugger that!" and they diverted their chartered Lockheed Electra to somewhere that was more welcoming.

And where did they escape to?

You are so clever: Key West, FL, 500 miles to the south of Jacksonville, and well out of harm's way of approaching Hurricane Dora.

The Beatles checked in to the Key Wester Motel next to the airport on South Roosevelt Blvd.

Here's a photo of what the Key Wester looked like back then: https://www.amazon.com/Wester-Florida-Original-Vintage-Postcard/dp/B071RY6LTL

And, no, that's not Gabrielle and me in the photo. Gabrielle was only five-years-old at the time, and I don't have those muscles…plus, I throw on shorts once I get within about 1500 miles of Key West.

BTW: The Key Wester was demolished in 1969 and the Hyatt Windward Pointe Resort now stands proudly in its gentrified place.

Next time you're down in Cayo Hueso, nip on over there to the Hyatt Windward Pointe and go out back to the open-air Tiki bar (the Beatles Hut it's colloquially called, as it was where the cottage the Beatles had stayed in had been located) and you will feast your eyes on the "Abbey Road Snack Shack," where the mop-tops knocked back the plonk, Vera, Chuck & Dave, and played and sang for the few other thrilled holidaymakers in attendance. When word hummed along the coconut grapevine that the Beatles were in Key West, a few local musicians flocked to the Key Wester after they got off work for the evening to jam, including Coffee Butler who was playing piano across the island at the old Hukilau (now—are you ready—the Homeland Security Office).

The night was young.

And humid.

The Beatles were shocked at how warm it still was late at night.

The most famous band in the world played for free brewskis and shots of tequila.

This from an interview that Paul McCartney did with *The Guardian* in 2004:

"We were in Key West in 1964. We were due to fly into Jacksonville, in Florida, and do a concert there, but we'd been diverted because of a hurricane. We stayed there (Key West) for a couple of days, not knowing what to do except, like, drink. I remember drinking way too much, and having one of those talking-to-the-toilet bowl evenings. It was during that night, when we'd all stayed up way too late, and we got so pissed that we ended up crying about, you know, how wonderful we were, and how much we loved each other, even though we'd never said anything. It was a good one: you never say anything like that. Especially if you're a Northern Man."

The concert back up at the Gator Bowl was held the day after Hurricane Dora struck, despite wide-ranging power outages in greater Jacksonville, 23,000 of the 32,000 fans who had scored on tickets attended.

The winds were swirling and still a very blustery 45 mph. Ringo's drum had to be nailed to the stage.

The concert's support acts were, in order of appearance: The Bill Black Combo, The Exciters, Clarence "Frogman" Henry, and Jackie DeShannon. There were 140 police officers on duty, and 84 firefighters acting as ushers to prevent fans from charging the stage.

The Beatles gyrated and had their hair blown back for a 12-song set: "Twist And Shout", "You Can't Do That", "All My Loving", "She Loves You", "Things We Said Today", "Roll Over Beethoven", "Can't Buy Me Love", "If I Fell", "I Want To Hold Your Hand", "Boys", "A Hard Day's Night," and "Long Tall Sally".

When John Lennon was asked if he was aware that President Johnson was in Jacksonville (to spurt political nonsense about hurricane recovery and get lots of air time), Lennon quipped: "Oh, he got a room, did he? We couldn't!"

FROM THE BEATLES' BIBLE, ref the concert in Jacksonville:

"We never play to segregated audiences and we aren't going to start now. I'd sooner lose out appearance money"—**John Lennon**

"We got on the plane to Jacksonville, Florida. But we found that there was a hurricane hitting Jacksonville, so they diverted us to Key West, announcing, 'Fasten your seat belts. The runaway isn't big enough for this plane. We're going to have to go in with full reverse thrust.' This was on an Electra, a plane that we later discovered has a very high accident record. But we landed at Key West all right and had our day off there"—**George Harrison**

"They said the hurricane had passed when we flew back into Jacksonville, but it was as windy as hell and it was dark with very heavy black clouds all over. It had cleared a bit, but there were still turbulent winds, and as we were approaching we could see the devastation: palm trees fallen over and mess laying everywhere"—**George Harrison**

**ACCIDENT INCIDENCE NOTE: Of the total of 170 Electras built, as of June 2011, 58 have been written off because of crashes and other accidents.

**WAIT THERE'S MORE: American Flyer Flight 280 was a flight operated on a U.S. Military Air Command contract from Monterey, California to Columbus, via Ardmore Municipal Airport in Oklahoma. On April 22, 1966, while approaching Runway 8 at Ardmore, the aircraft overshot the runway and crashed into a hill, bursting into flames. Eighty-three of the 98 passengers and crew on board died as a result of the accident.

The aircraft was a Lockheed Electra L-188 four-engine turboprop airline registered as *N183H*.

It was the same plane that the Beatles had chartered to fly from city to city during their second tour of the U.S.

The doomed plane was piloted by the president of American Flyers Airline, Reed Pigman. Cause of the crash was determined to be cardiac arrest of Pigman.

AND THIS FROM CONCERT-GOERS:

"I was at this concert. I recall the disappointment because the wind was blowing the Beatles' hair back and their show stopping haircuts weren't visible. I was seated on the ground, not too far from the stage. However, I could barely make out the words of any song due to the number of screaming females in the audience. It was insane! I don't recall the number of opening acts listed here. I only remember one and that was a female group. I wish there was a poster to commemorate this event. I lost my tickets years ago."

"Yes, I was there, along with a friend. I was 15 years old. It was a very emotional experience for me. My dad drove us about 2 hours each way, on a rainy night. The fact that he was willing to do this is just a memorable as the actual concert. Wish I had kept my ticket stubs."

"I was there. My poor mother took 7 teenage girls and 1 guy from Gainesville to Jacksonville for the concert. It was unreal for a 14 year old to attend that kind of show."

Meanwhile, back down in Key West, Beatlemania was rampant and the water from the swimming pool where the Beatles lounged and swam and peed, was bottled and sold. Even the bedsheets that the Beatles had slept on were cut into one-square-inch strips and, along with an affidavit of authenticity outlining which Beatle had slept on which sheet, were sold.

The small vials of water from the swimming pool cost more than the actual tickets to the concert.

The swatches of bedsheet?

Priceless.

**THIS JUST IN: Gabrielle and I were talking to our friend John Rubin the other day. Remember him from my Key West books? The guy who works in the film and music business and looks like Alfred Hitchcock? The guy who's always in Key West for the fishing? The guy who as a young boy smuggled a chicken into a showing of Hitchcock's *THE BIRDS* and then let it loose from the balcony during the flappy part of the movie? Yes, that's him.

Anyhoo, John Rubin was good friends with impresario Sid Bernstein. Bernstein changed the American music scene in the 1960s by bringing The Beatles, the Rolling Stones, Herman's Hermits, the Moody Blues, and the Kinks to America. He was the first concert promoter to organize rock concerts at sports stadiums.

Bernstein persuaded Brian Epstein that The Beatles could be successful in the US, and booked them into Carnegie Hall for their first appearance without informing the venue of their style of music.

The Beatles performed two sellout concerts at Carnegie Hall, this would be just three days after that historic appearance on *The Ed Sullivan Show*.

After the shows at Carnegie Hall, when The Beatles had finished, the dust had settled, the cleaning crew found that nearly every seat in Carnegie Hall was soaked with urine.

Sid Bernstein was told that The Beatles would not be welcomed back.

CHAPTER 17—Willie Nelson

Over the years, there have been many sightings of Willie Nelson in Key West, none confirmed by anyone sober.

Many folk swear up and down that they've seen the former Bible salesman hanging out in the Green Parrot, problem with that supposition is there's often a shitload of Willie Nelson doppelgangers who drink in the Green Parrot.

And, no, the gravestone at the Key West cemetery that has "Willie Nelson" engraved on it has nothing to do with our Willie.

Hop on your bike and ride on over to the cemetery, pardner, see if you can find it, and you'll see why.

Then, go back to the Green Parrot.

Go late.

CHAPTER 18—Harris Glenn Milstead

Who?

Perhaps you know him better as "Divine"?

Divine starred in the original movie of *Hairspray* (1988) playing Ricki Lake's ("Tracy Turnblad") mother Edna Turnblad.

You will recall that the role was later revived by John Travolta in the 2007 *Hairspray* remake.

On account of Divine playing the role in drag, the role in all future productions was cast with a male.

Divine was the king of, well, Drag Queens, and performed at The Copa (623 Duval) in the late 70s…long before it burned down (in 1995), although, when he/she was here, the show apparently was quite hot unto itself.

Divine enjoyed being carried onstage by six macho, well-oiled, well-muscled brick shithouses.

And he brought down the house with his inimitable version of "Walk like a Man," "Born to be Cheap," and "Shoot Your Shot."

Quotes can say a lot about an individual. Here are a few from divine:

"All my life I wanted to look like Elizabeth Taylor. Now Elizabeth Taylor looks like me."

"People who used to make fun are now fans. I had the last laugh."

"Of course the last thing my parents wanted was a son who wears a cocktail dress that glitters, but they've come around to it."

"My favorite part of dressing in drag is getting out of it. Drag is my work clothes. I only put it on when someone pays me to."

"I think I've always been respectable. What I do onstage is not what I do in my private life...It's an act...It's how I make my living. People laugh, and it's not hurting anyone."

"People like to be shocked...and that was my job to get out there and shock them..."

Divine's death shocked everyone.

Divine weighed nearly 400 pounds when he died in 1988 at the young age of 42 from cardiac arrest brought on by a combination of cardiomegaly, obesity, and sleep apnea. His doctor had warned him to cut down his food intake and not to sleep on his back.

Divine used to pull up a chair and sit in front of his refrigerator with the door open.

He remains a cult figure to this day.

CHAPTER 19—Grace Jones

Grace Jones came to Key West and played The Copa in the late 70s, as well.

Jones was born in Jamaica and she found the island "gender expression" ambience of Cayo Hueso back then much to her liking.

**AUTHOR'S HISTORICAL NOTE: The Copa in the mid-80s was a popular gay-oriented dance club and *the* place to see and be seen and be, well, *you*.

The Copa hosted grand theme parties, and there was always a long line waiting for the doors to open. "Pinkie" worked the ticket window, "Ray" worked the door and if you were fortunate enough to actually gain entry, you made a bee line for "naughtiness" in the form of The Garden Bar. It was out back here where decadence reigned supreme.

A suspicious fire in 1995 brought the place to its knees (if you'll excuse the turn of phrase).

But what a way to go!

Fifty-foot flames were licking The Copa, hunky fireman fought valiantly, and the music was still pounding out from within!

More than 100 patrons at The Copa, plus the terrified, panicking tenants at the apartment upstairs, and a nearby rooming house had to be evacuated.

And boy did they ever evacuate.

CHAPTER 20—John Waters

Waters was once quoted as saying: "I wanted to make the trashiest motion pictures in cinema history."

Waters is the self-proclaimed "Pope of Trash," and an Independent, Underground Filmmaker who first made a name for himself with a series of low budget, filthy, campy, outrageous shorts, and then hit it big with the Box Office smash-hit and cult-classic *Hairspray*.

TIP O' DAY: If you are able to climb off the hamster wheel for the Christmas holidays and just happen to be down here on the rock, pop on over and catch his profanity-laced, critically acclaimed one-man show, cleverly entitled: **A JOHN WATERS CHRISTMAS SHOW.**

From *KEYS WEEKLY*. "I love going to places like Florida that are not thought of as Christmassy," said Waters, who has a long history with Key West. Waters stayed with friend, muse and star of many of his movies, the infamous Miss Divine, in Key West while writing parts of his bestselling book *Shock Value* (1981). In 2013, Waters returned to headline the Key West Film Festival for the documentary feature *I Am Divine*, about the beloved friend and drag queen…"

And now below, please find a few questions posed to John Waters regarding his friend "Divine," and his one-man show, followed by his answers:

What was your favorite thing about Divine?

"His kindness and his generosity."

What's your fondest memory of him?

"He really loved Christmas, so seeing him really happy in one of his great homes with all of the great food that he loved to make that eventually killed him."

What is your favorite thing about being on stage?

"I get to tour the world and meet my audience, and I have the coolest audience in the world—and they dress great."

John Waters is charismatic, endearing, witty, cheeky, irreverent and more than just a bit naughty.

If you get a chance to see him live, Go!

And prepare to be offended.

CHAPTER 21—Steven Spielberg

I'm having trouble verifying if Spielberg actually set foot in flippo-floppos on our shores, but I will just tell you this: His 282-foot private yacht the *Seven Seas* (named for his *seven* kids) was spotted off Key West, but then again, perhaps it was just being chartered. Spielberg does that, you know, charters his yacht. Only $1.2 million per month, as if he needs the dosh.

He's worth $3.7 billion.

Do you remember the line from the movie *Jaws*? The one where Chief Brody almost gets a facial from the shark while he's chumming and falters back, cigarette dangling from quivering lips, and quips: "You're gonna need a bigger boat!"

Well, director Steven Spielberg must have taken the line to heart as he's just placed an order to have a new super yacht built. It will only be 18-feet longer, but that means *she* will have hit the coveted "300-foot threshold," which apparently is a very big deal in yachting circles.

Oh, pray tell, HOW MUCH will this new toy cost? you ask.

An out of this world, something to phone home about, cool $250 million.

Here's a video of his "old" super yacht churning away from the quay in Ft. Lauderdale. No, it's not the marvelous white boat on the left, rather the monster blue mega-yacht on the right, thrusting sideways.

Watch how long it takes them to get the fenders up.

https://www.youtube.com/watch?v=3twIloLrdVo

Oh, and just for old time's sake, here's a link to that scene in *Jaws*, "You're gonna need a bigger boat!"

https://www.youtube.com/watch?v=2I91DJZKRxs

CHAPTER 22—Jack Nicholson

Here's a video that some schmuck shot illicitly of dear Jack (and a whole lot of other crap) as Jack was endeavoring to quietly browse in a Duval Street T-shirt shop: https://www.youtube.com/watch?v=LmRFK0-xVcw

Did you take a peek at the video?

If you haven't had the chance yet, I will just tell you that Jack was mulling over parting with a microscopic amount of his staggering $390 million-dollar fortune to purchase a lonely T-shirt.

Now this begs two questions:

#1 Why buy a T-shirt when you are known for running around your house stark-buck naked?

WT-bleeping-F?

From *Work + Money*: "Jack Nicholson once wandered around his home completely nude for several months…and he didn't put on clothes for anyone. Seriously. While interviewing Nicholson for *Rolling Stone*, journalist Erik Hedegaard remarked about the surreal experience while he was at Nicholson's house: '…he once spent three months walking around in the nude, at all hours of the day, no matter who stopped by, his daughter included.

'…he walked around nude for quite a while in order to get used to appearing nude in a film for a sex scene. While filming, Nicholson said he went upstairs and tried to get an erection for 45 minutes for a scene in *The Postman Always Rings Twice*…'"

#2 Perhaps the T-shirt had a cool painting on it, designed by one of the talented Key West artists? Jack Nicholson is known to be a connoisseur of art, as he's one of Hollywood's biggest art collectors, with his collection worth $100 million.

Not related at all to Key West, but fascinating and I just have to put it in here because of local musician Al Subarsky: Jack

Nicholson and Danny DeVito's parents owned a hair salon together on Jersey's "Irish Riviera" at 505 Mercer Avenue.

Jack Nicholson was a lifeguard at a local beach.

Danny DeVito worked at the hair salon shampooing women's hair.

Contrary to rumor, Jack and Danny did NOT grow up together as little kids. Nicholson was seven years older and they didn't meet until they hit Hollywood.

You may remember they were both in *One Flew Over the Cuckoo's Nest* (produced by DeVito's former roommate, Michael Douglas, no less).

Nicholson won his first Oscar for the role of a mental patient in *One Flew over the Cuckoo's Nest*. Gene Hackman, Burt Reynolds, Marlon Brando, and James Caan were each offered the role, but they all turned it down.

Who knew?

CHAPTER 23—Tom Corcoran

If you would've loved to have been a fly on the wall in Key West back in the 70s, you would've loved to have been Tom Corcoran.

Author of the contagious and best-selling Alex Rutledge mysteries. An all-around cool guy, Ford Mustang aficionado, former magazine editor, present publisher, renowned photographer (his photographs have appeared on 7 album covers for Jimmy Buffett, and book covers for James W. Hall and Tom McGuane), and he co-wrote the Buffett hits "Cuban Crime of Passion" and "Fins," and two screenplays with Hunter S. Thompson.

All that plus he's a gentleman with a killer sense of humor.

Tom has lived the life that we all wish we could have lived…or at least have ridden shotgun. Listen to what he says here: "I lived among pot smugglers, financial scammers, people with false identities, and wealthy people with bad habits and powerful failings."

I don't know about you, but I don't *want to be like Mike,* I want to be like Tom.

The thing I like about Tom Corcoran is that in many ways he represents what Key West is all about. He's a sterling example of someone who came to the island, embraced all that it offered, let the creative juices pervade his soul and BANG! made something of himself.

Our Tom first came to Key West with the Navy in the late 60s and was smitten by what he saw: palm trees doing the Lambada, Tanqueray-clear waters, and a seductive island life-style. When his stint in the Navy was complete, Tom returned to Key West. He had no job, no money…but he had guts, he was intrepid…and he had dreams of being a writer.

This is how it is for many.

You reinvent yourself.

You reach deep down inside and find out talents, skill, knacks, that you didn't even know you had.

This is how it was for Gabrielle and me. We arrived, no jobs, no money, but, we too, were smitten and we had to reinvent ourselves.

The same for Popcorn Joe.

And Will Soto.

And The Cookie Lady.

And the original Joke Man.

Knife Sharpening Man

Dominique the Catman.

And many others who simply turned up on the rock looking as if they'd just stepped off the boat and realized they were "home to a place they'd never been before."

Tom Corcoran got creative. He was graced with a photographer's eye, he soon saw a niche and he set out to fill it—with tacos.

Whaaat?

Yes, tacos.

You don't need a car in Key West, not that Tom could've afforded one, so he acquired a three-wheeled bicycle.

And he pedaled up and down Duval, past all the watering holes and even to the beaches and he sold his tacos—three for a dollar.

He even sold tacos to Tennessee Williams and his crowd of hangers-on.

The tacos were a hit.

Tom was a hit.

Tom was also friendly, personable, likeable, respectful. He made contacts, he made friends. And, he was easy to spot coming down the street on his three-wheeled bicycle—the man is six-feet-five and sports a ten-gallon smile.

Once settled, Tom rang his girlfriend back up in the Great White North and said something to the effect of "Stop doing what you're doing and get down here, you won't believe this place."

Tom's girlfriend had a prestigious job and a parent (her

father) who was difficult to please and kept short reins. There was no way she could just chuck it all into the wind and jump ship.

But she did.

She gave it all up, moved to Key West and got a job tending bar at Capt. Tony's.

And life was good.

And then it got better. Tom became the bartender at the Pier House's Chart Room Bar.

Key West in the early 70s was an idyllic aerie. A naughty backwater with little in the way of traditional law and order.

You could say the Chart Room Bar was much the same. The bar was small, once a former hotel room, darkly lit, moody, five or six barstools hogging the bar, holes drilled in the transom and filled with the ashes of deceased regulars, then plugged.

It's where good and evil rubbed shoulders.

It's where politicians met and struck deals.

It's where dealers dealt.

Dreams were dreamt.

And then one day, two young men walked in. The tall fellow knew Tom and greeted him warmly. The shorter fellow was all blond tussled-hair and smiles—but he looked like he needed a hug.

Tom looked at the sad soul and said "Welcome to Key West, first beer's on me."

And that's all the hug a young Jimmy Buffett needed. And he thanked his friend Jerry Jeff Walker for dragging him into the Chart Room Bar to meet Tom.

Later, Tom knew that Jimmy Buffett was struggling to make ends meet…struggling to even eat.

So he took him home for some home-cooked spaghetti.

As one should.

And a life-long friendship was formed.

Tom Corcoran, with a photographer's keen observing-eye and his pulse on the heart, soul and underbelly of Cayo Hueso from his perch tending bar at the infamous Chart Room.

With that pedigree, he was destined to become a writer.

And are we ever glad he did.

**BTW: As mentioned, Tom Corcoran has his own publishing company and they have a lot of cool books on offer. Here it is right in front of your face. Check it out: www.tomcorcoran.net/kyindex.html

CHAPTER 24—James W. Hall

Along with Tom Corcoran, James W. Hall is one of my favorite writers.

Did you know JWH taught at Florida International University in Miami for 40 years, where he was a full professor of Literature *and* founded the school's Creative Writing program in the early 1970s?

Professor Hall—has a nice ring to it, wouldn't you agree?

I would've loved to have been in that Creative Writing program, but I missed the boat. Not anywhere near the port, actually. Having said that, James W. Hall did pen a non-fiction book in 2012 about the "12 essential elements that make up a bestseller," and I've got my twitchy little hands on that very book now.

So I continue to learn.

The book is cleverly entitled ***Hit Lit: Cracking the Code of the Twentieth Century's Biggest Bestsellers***.

In this book James W. Hall "reveals how bestsellers work, using twelve twentieth-century blockbusters as case studies, such as: *The Godfather, Gone with the Wind, To Kill a Mockingbird,* and *Jaws*. From tempting glimpses inside secret societies, such as submariners in *The Hunt for Red October,* and Opus Dei in *The Da Vinci Code,* to vivid representations of the American Dream and its opposite—the American Nightmare—in novels like *The Firm* and *The Dead Zone,* Hall identifies the common features of mega-bestsellers. Including fascinating and little-known facts about some of the most beloved books of the last century…"

The man clearly understands the nuances of writing and is a maven of Literature. Check this out: Hanging on the wall in his office above his coveted roll-top desk is a Master's Degree in Creative Writing from prestigious John Hopkins University in Baltimore and a Doctorate in Literature from the University of

Utah.

And…he was a Fulbright Professor of Literature in Spain, as well.

**FYI: "The Fulbright is a United States Cultural Exchange Program whose goal is to improve intercultural relations and cultural diplomacy between the people of the United States and other countries through the exchange of persons, knowledge, and skills. It is one of the most prestigious and competitive fellowship programs in the world. Via the program, competitively-selected American citizens including students, scholars, teachers, professionals, scientists and artists may receive scholarships or grants to study, conduct research, teach, or exercise their talents abroad.

"The program was founded by US Senator J. William Fulbright in 1946 and is considered to be one of the most widely recognized and prestigious scholarships in the world."

* * *

I don't know about you Dear Reader, but I'm sincerely impressed.

Possibly even more impressed when I learned James W. Hall had designs on being a professional tennis player.

In JWH's own words: "I wanted to be a professional tennis player. But as a senior in high school, I had the misfortune of playing a younger kid from a nearby prep school, a ninth-grade hick. I should whoop his butt, right? Turns out it was Roscoe Tanner. Future Wimbledon finalist. So much for that dream."

All that above, right there in black and white on his curriculum vitae. Not bad for someone who started out slaving away in grubby kitchens, planting gi-normous palm trees around condominium blocks, working as a lifeguard, toiling as a gofer in a marina washing yachts, slicing roast beef in a buffet greasy spoon, working as a mechanic at a go-kart track, working as a ranch hand at Robert Redford's Sundance Resort ("which means I built a fence for him with some other guys"), and acting as a camp counselor up in the mountains of North Carolina.

There's nothing wrong with humble beginnings.

James W. Hall, PhD., is an Edgar and Shamus Award-winning author whose books have been translated into twelve languages. As of this printing, he has written twenty novels, four books of poetry, a collection of short stories, and a collection of essays.

He also won a John D. MacDonald Award for Excellence in Florida Fiction, presented by the JDM Bibliophile.

The New York Times calls him "the master of suspense," the *San Francisco Chronicle* pegs him as "brilliant" and Michael Connelly—no slouch as a crime novelist himself—readily acknowledges Hall's influence on his own writing, saying that Hall's "people and places have more brushstrokes than a Van Gogh."

His students up at Florida International University have included Dennis Lehane. You might recognize the name "Dennis Lehane" from his novels *Gone, Baby, Gone*, which was adapted into a film in 2007 and directed by Ben Affleck; *Mystic River* adapted into a film in 2003 and directed by Clint Eastwood; and *Shutter Island* adapted into a 2010 film and directed by Martin Scorsese.

James W. Hall lived along Blackwater Sound in Key Largo for many years and can still be spied down here in Key West researching sights, sounds and smells for a bestseller or as a guest lecturer at the Key West Literary Seminar.

If you want to sink your choppers into a good crime/thriller set in Key West, check out his killer-thriller entitled: *Bones of Coral.*

Here's a short synopsis: "A Key West thriller featuring the creepiest, scariest, funniest bad guy ever. Dougie Barnes has no pain threshold and he loves a good rhyme. Paramedic Shaw Chandler knows Miami's nitty-gritty all too well. But when a routine suicide call uncovers his long-lost father, it's anything but routine-and it appears it's anything but suicide. Then Shaw's mother falls victim to financial fraud, leaving Shaw with no choice but to return home to Key West and into the arms of his old flame soap opera actress Trula Montoya. Trula's got her own skeletons and reasons for returning to Key West. Rekindling her relationship to Shaw can only complicate her life. But Trula and

Shaw are about to learn that they can no longer run from their secrets or the past as they discover a lethal conspiracy and science run amok. And when a psychotic, rhyming killer is added to the mix, they must stop an evil that could spell doom to all."

It is a damn good read.

CHAPTER 25—Carl Hiaasen

Of Norwegian descent, Hiaasen has a wicked sense of humor (just like Tom Corcoran and James W. Hall).

It helps to have a sense of humor if you live in Florida.

The surname "Hiaasen" comes from the name of a farm in Sigdal, Norway (population 3,509), not all that far from Oslo. Really, really far from the offices of the *Miami Herald*, and even farther from Key West.

Hiaasen's writing genre has been pleasantly called "sunshine noir." So very clever.

"I probably couldn't write the novels I write if I didn't have at least one toe in the newsroom," Hiaasen has noted. "This constant over-the-transom flow of sleaze inspires the novels."

I just love that. A writer needs to understand the importance of the sleaze factor.

Hiaasen has been a guest speaker at the literary festival here on the island, as well. If you see his name listed for an upcoming festival, don't tarry, the tickets go fast.

Check out his book *Bad Monkey*. It's set in Key West and Big Pine Key.

CHAPTER 26—Tennessee Williams

Tennessee Williams' father was a traveling salesman, a drunk, and a brawling bully (he had a portion of his ear bitten off in a poker fight).

When Tennessee's father tired of the traveling, he came home to roost, secured a local job and saw a lot more of his son Tennessee, and as Tennessee himself recounted: "…my father began to see more of me…and he didn't like what he saw."

In his father's eyes, Tennessee was not what he had hoped for in a little boy, so he verbally abused and humiliated him by calling him "Miss Nancy."

Tennessee's mother was much the opposite of his father. His mother was prim, puritanical and a teetotaler. She had a fear of touching and a hatred of sex.

"She used to scream every time she had sex with my father," recalled Tennessee, "and we children were terrified. We'd run out in the streets and the neighbors would take us in."

The tension and dysfunction at home greatly unsettled Tennessee's fragile, older sister "Rose," and she became increasingly delusional.

"Rose is liable to go down and get a butcher knife one night and cut your throat," warned a psychiatrist. This diagnosis freaked Tennessee's mother out, so in 1943 (when Rose was 24), she forced her only daughter to undergo a bilateral, pre-frontal lobotomy, one of the first performed in America at the time. The removal of the pre-frontal cortex of her brain apparently was not enough, and Rose had to endure and suffer through 19 terrifying years of electric-shock treatment.

Rose would remain a virgin all her life.

In 1967, lobotomy was banned in the United States.

* * *

When he first arrived in Key West, in 1941, at the age of 30, Tennessee stayed in an antebellum boarding house on Duval Street.

Later, after time away from the island spent in New Orleans where he wrote most of *A Streetcar Named Desire*, he returned to Key West and resided in a two-room, top-floor suite at La Concha Hotel. It was here, with that glorious view, that he worked in peace and finally finished *Streetcar*.

But the peace didn't last long.

Visiting tourons, who were doing their damnedest to become proficient in the Duval Crawl, would spot the now famous playwright coming and going or simply standing out front sucking on a fag, and they would approach like a pack of hyenas, introduce themselves, want to shake his hand, and perhaps even snag an autograph.

So Tennessee went house hunting and eventually found a quant, tin-roofed, red-shuttered cottage at 1431 Duncan Street in a more secluded and tranquil area on the fringe of the Old Town known as The Meadows.

Williams put his stamp on the property by transforming it into a modest compound that included a guest house, a swimming pool (with an inlaid tiled rose mosaic on the bottom), and a one-room writing studio that he called the "Mad House."

Away from Duval, but not away from hate: Half the island knew that Tennessee hung out at a renowned gay disco called "The Monster" (like its namesake on Fire Island) and at the Pier House, at the time just a motel and popular with the era's gay community.

Within a matter of months, Tennessee's gay gardener (a bejeweled eccentric man fond of shrieking "I am a sick woman!") was brutally murdered, and his own house ransacked multiple times. Tennessee was mugged twice walking home in Key West's Old Town. His beloved bulldog mysteriously vanished from the face of the earth. And a gaggle of unruly local youths stood outside his house, throwing beer cans at the front door while yelling "Come on out, faggot!"

CRIME SCENE NOTE: The police officer dispatched to the murder scene of Tennessee Williams' gardener (who resided in the Railroad Museum's living quarters) filed this chilling report: "I walked inside the door and observed the victim naked (except for a pair of white socks). Victim was lying on his back just inside the doorway, a small hole above right ear, and another small hole below left side of neck. A large amount of blood was coming out of the victim's nose, also victim was lying in a large pool of blood which was partially coagulated. Upon checking victim's pulse and breathing I found he was already dead."

Despite the murder, despite the beatings, despite the homophobic hate, Williams remained fiercely proud of what he was, and who he was.

He had come to the Southernmost City to write and to swim, and he wasn't going anywhere anytime soon.

Thomas Lanier Williams, III, was born 26 March 1911 in Columbus, Mississippi. When he was 28, Williams moved to New Orleans and adapted the moniker "Tennessee."

When interviewed by Dick Cavett in 1974 why he didn't end up using the name "Mississippi Williams" instead of Tennessee, he responded: "My friends call me 'Tenn' Williams, now what would they call me if I was called Mississippi Williams?"

AUTHOR'S NOTE: Back when Tennessee was a young man, in the early to middle 1930s, he went by the name of Tom Williams when he put pen to paper and wrote poetry and short stories. But then as success came, he endeavored to find a more appropriate pen name. He had considered "Valentine Xavier," but eventually decided that it "seemed a bit pompous." Then he felt his new name should at least match the initials for Tom Williams, so he settled on "Tennessee."

Why? you ask.

I will tell you right now. He had a strong ancestral attachment to the state of Tennessee: one relative had been a senator from Tennessee (and friend of Davy Crockett), another had served three terms in the U.S. House of representatives, and a third, had run (unsuccessfully) for governor of Tennessee *four* times.

So "Tennessee" it was to be.

* * *

Williams was pretty much an unknown playwright until he received unrivalled success with his production of *The Glass Menagerie*, then his career really took off with *A Streetcar Named Desire*, *Cat on a Hot Tin Roof*, *The Night of the Iguana* (not inspired by the invasive denizens that now roam Key West), *Sweet Bird of Youth*, and of course *The Rose Tattoo*.

As with many individuals of an artistic temperament, Tennessee Williams sought inspiration, freedom, and relief from mental health issues by upping sticks, committing social suicide, and changing locals. He spent lengths of time in New Orleans, New York, Sitges (a picturesque-beachside gay enclave just south of Barcelona), Rome and London.

But he always returned to Key West.

There was something in the air...in the water...in the locals that spurred him on, motivated him and satiated him. He said, "I work everywhere, but I work best here."

Williams lived in his cozy bungalow on Duncan Street with his lover Frank Merlo a sometimes actor and fulltime alcoholic. Williams was an alcoholic, as well, and he and Merlo were heavily into recreational and prescription drugs: blow, speed, and downers.

Frank Merlo an American-Italian muscleman and former sailor became Tennessee Williams' personal secretary, his confidant, his wall upon which to bounce ideas. Merlo's presence in Tennessee Williams' life brought a degree of stability to the mercurial writer and it shooed away the demons that tortured Tennessee with fears of descending into mental illness hell, as had befallen his sister.

The romance between Tennessee and Frank lasted for fourteen years until ripped apart and destroyed by infidelity and drug abuse.

Through it all, Tennessee continued to carry a torch for Frank Merlo and when Merlo died of lung cancer in 1963, Williams slipped off the edge of the earth and fell into a bottomless chasm of depression, and his alcohol and drug abuse went AWOL.

Williams was treated for his depression by a certain Dr. Max

71

Jacobson. The good doctor was also known by his stable of celebrity patients as "Dr. Feelgood," or "Miracle Max."

Tennessee was repeatedly injected with a drug regime colloquially referred to as "fire shots." Fire shots were a cocktail of amphetamines, painkillers, vitamins and even human placenta. On occasion, Tennessee would complement the injections with Mellaril (an anti-psychotic) and chase it with whiskey. Where the short-term effect may have been impressive, the long-term result was less so, and Tennessee had to be frequently hospitalized and even committed to mental health facilities.

PHARMACEUTICAL NOTE: Mellaril, taken together with alcohol can cause uncontrollable movements, agitation, seizures, severe dizziness or fainting, coma, very deep sleep, irregular heartbeats, and high or low body temperature.

Dr. Max Jacobson had a laundry list of celebrities, including Marlene Dietrich, Truman Capote, Gore Vidal, Rod Sterling, Marilyn Monroe, President Kennedy, Jacqueline Kennedy, Cecil B. DeMille, Winston Churchill, Elvis Presley, Liz Taylor, Richard Burton, Anthony Quinn, Judy Garland, Eddie Fisher, Andy Williams, Johnny Mathis, Yul Brynner and Andy Warhol.

The comfort Williams found in Key West would not sustain him in the end. In his 2014 biography of Williams, author John Lahr wrote: "The playwright fled Key West in turmoil over the fact that his new work was not connecting with the public."

Leonica McGee, his housekeeper in Key West at the time, recalls hearing him call a taxi. According to Lahr, "When she inquired about the car, he told her that he was going to New York. She asked when he'd be coming back. 'I won't ever be coming home again,' he said."

LINK NOTE: Here's a great photo of Leonica McGee with David Wolkowsky in 1986.
https://www.kwls.org/archive/1986/attachment/1986-mcgee-wolkowsky/

On February 25, 1983, Tennessee Williams was found dead in his suite at the Hotel Elysée, New York City, by his personal assistant John Uecker. Uecker had been asleep in the adjoining room on the night that Williams died. Uecker said he had heard a noise in Tennessee's room sometime before midnight, but did not investigate. The next morning, Uecker knocked on the door which lead to Tennessee's room, but received no response. He knocked again. Nothing. Finally, he went in and found Tennessee Williams sprawled on the floor next to his bed.

An empty bottle of wine and containers of assorted prescription drugs were found on the nightstand.

New York City's chief medical examiner, Dr. Elliot Gross, performed an autopsy and the cause of death was listed as asphyxia due to obstruction of the glottis (the opening to the larynx or upper airway) by a plastic over-cap (of the type used to cover the opening of nasal spray or ophthalmic solution dispenser). He went on to say that "further studies, including chemical tests, would be performed."

The police were unable to say what the bottle cap might have belonged to. "All the medication was taken from the apartment by the Medical Examiner's office," said Captain Gene Burke of the Manhattan detective squad. "We don't have any information on it."

When the chemical test results came back, tissue samples confirmed the presence of secobarbital and alcohol in Tennessee Williams' system.

This scenario left the general public wondering what really transpired, and folk began to question the official account of Williams' death.

Forensic detective and expert Michael Baden reviewed the medical files in regards to Tennessee's death, and stated that the results showed that he died of a drug and alcohol overdose, not from choking. Williams' friend playwright Larry Myers said that the autopsy report was later modified to state that Williams actually died of acute Seconal intolerance, and Tennessee's Key West friend Scott Kenan stated that someone in the coroner's office had invented the bottle cap scenario.

Purportedly, Dr. Gross later acknowledged the bottle cap would not have been large enough to restrict airflow. Gross was certain that the event that had caused Tennessee's death was inadvertent. He filed a false report stating that the playwright had died by choking on a medicine bottle top. He had surmised that if the Press, clamoring loudly outside the hotel, heard that drugs had been part of the cause of death, they would report it as an overdose or suicide—an unjust verdict—but one that would live in the mind of the public forever.

Hmm, difficult to know what to believe here.

In Tennessee Williams' Last Will and Testament, written in 1972, he requested to be buried at sea, "sewn up in a clean white sack and dropped overboard 12 hours north of Havana." This was where 33-year-old poet Hart Crane—whose work Williams had admired since childhood—jumped to his death from a cruise ship. (Witnesses heard Crane say "Goodbye everybody," as he hurled himself into the Atlantic.)

Upon hearing of Tennessee Williams' death, the old Picture Show movie house at 620 Duval Street, now long closed down, screened *The Rose Tattoo* non-stop throughout the afternoon and evening. Fans lined up outside and crowded into the theater. The cinema was packed all night long, and many in the audience sat through two showings.

AUTHOR'S CELLULOID NOTE: The Picture Show was a converted storefront theater. During the day, they screened "The Key West Picture Show," a 40-minute travelogue for tourists. At night, they transformed into a repertory theater, showing alternative and cult films.

Tennessee Williams was 71 years old when he passed.

CHAPTER 27—Al Capone

Al Capone aka "Scarface" wintered in Miami Beach at his 14-room secluded retreat on Palm Island. The island is located in the middle of Biscayne Bay between downtown Miami and South Beach, and accessible by the MacArthur Causeway. Capone had purchased the property at 93 Palm Avenue, in 1928, for $40,000 from none other than beer magnate August Busch. This just happened to be right in the middle of Prohibition, in case you were wondering.

What do you think?

Coincidence?

* * *

If Scarface had the urge to pay a visit to Cuba, he would fly by private seaplane direct from Miami. And on occasion, he would make his way down to Key West and use the backwater island as a stopover and less-visual departure point on his way to Havana.

Capone fancied La Concha Hotel on Duval. How could you not?

Can you imagine if you're down here from the Great White North and you're staying at La Concha, as well, and you end up sitting next to him at the bar, and after a few too many, and in spite of the white fedora, the Cuban cigar, and accompanying gorillas, you don't recognize Big Al. Perhaps, in a giddy mood from the three mojitos you just knocked back after all that beer, you turn to him and say: "So…what do you do?"

Of course Al Capone groans, but you are now feeling quite chatty and want some company, what with the Mrs not there to talk her ear off (the Mrs is upstairs listening to Arthur Godfrey on the wireless).

So, you sort of blurt out: "Just down here killing time?"

And you don't notice that the gorillas have just reached

inside their suit jackets (suit jackets on a sultry, stifling hot evening).

Still bent on initiating conversation, you then sputter: "Geez, those awful scars on your face, you should get that looked at!"

When this doesn't initiate intercourse, and you are now encircled by the gorillas, you hold up your fourth mojito and chortle (yes, chortle) "Cheers and up yours!" Then you elbow him and cackle (yes, cackle): "Boy, I'm sure glad prohibition's over, what say you, bud?"

UNDERWORLD NOTE: During Prohibition, Capone was the first gangster to set up business in Cuba, with both Lucky Luciano and Meyer Lansky, making frequent trips from Miami, or Key West, to Havana to oversee their bootlegging operations.

Now get upstairs and spend some quality time with the little Mrs and Arthur Godfrey before the gorillas escort you down to the harbor and you go swimming with the fishes.

CHAPTER 28—Meyer Lansky

Much like Al Capone, Lanksy would on occasion embark for Havana from the island of Key West.

Europeans and Americans were flocking to Havana for the beaches, brothels (Havana used to be known as "the whorehouse of the Caribbean,") the rum, the big bands, and Cuban cigars.

And, yes, the gambling.

But the casinos were being stolen blind by the non-Cuban croupiers and dealers, and the games were getting a bad reputation, so tourists began to take their expendable cash to the casinos in Puerto Rico, instead.

Enter Meyer Lansky, the *accountant* to the mob, the *fixer*, and himself a shrewd mobster.

El Presidente Fulgencio Batista got wind of Lansky's reputation and went to him for help.

Meyer Lansky may have only been five-feet tall on a good day, but he had muscle, and he knew how to lean on people.

Long story, short, Lansky enacted reform: dealers and croupiers—most of them American—who were crooked, were deported and a new practice of dealing Blackjack from a six-deck shoe was implemented. This helped the house in terms of percentage and minimized cheating by both the dealers and players.

Batista was impressed and a mutually beneficial arrangement came about in which the American Mafia was to share the profits from all future casinos, hotels, and nightclubs with Batista, his inner circle, and senior Cuban Army and police officers. In return, Cuban authorities allowed the Mafia to operate its establishments without interference. Over the next twenty-five years, a gangster state took root in Cuba as Batista, other corrupt Cuban politicians, and senior Cuban army and police officers lined their pockets.

And Americans came to Miami and Key West to take the ferries over, or fly on Pan Am.

Do you remember the character "Hyman Roth," portrayed by Lee Strasberg, in *The Godfather Part II* (1974)?

Roth's character was based on Meyer Lansky.

CHAPTER 29—The Rev. Morris Wright

Okay, Dear Reader, I will only be the messenger here, you be the judge:

On Jan. 12, 1979, Rev. Morris Wright, the minister at the Key West Baptist Temple on Stock Island, placed an advertisement in The Key West *Citizen*, in which he called on the County Commissioner to "help bring back some of the uniqueness of the Key West and the Florida Keys way of life."

"If I were the chief of police," wrote Rev. Wright, "I would get me a hundred good men, give them each a baseball bat and have them walk down Duval Street and dare one of these freaks to stick his head over the edge of the sidewalk."

He continued, "That is the way it was done in Key West in the days I remember and loved. Female impersonators and queers were loaded into a deputy's automobile and shipped to the county line."

This Ad placed in the local rag we fondly refer to as the Mullet Wrap urged readers to "root out sodomites."

And a series of anti-gay crimes followed.

Anti-gay activist and famous singer and spokeswoman Anita Bryant had promised to come down to Key West to support the reverend and aid his crusade.

Bryant referred to gays as "human garbage."

Anita Bryant had essentially been the "face of Florida orange juice," so gay bartenders in Key West, and around America, boycotted Florida orange juice and concocted Screwdrivers with apple juice instead.

The name of this new drink? you ask.

It was called the "Anita Bryant."

Perhaps I should have saved the Rev. for my book on "closed-minded, uneducated, homophobic hate-mongers."

Just saying.

CHAPTER 30—Burt Lancaster

Burt Lancaster was born on November 2nd, 1913, in the slums of East Harlem. Depending on the direction of the wind, East Harlem residents were assaulted by the stench from breweries, coal yards, saw mills and slaughter houses. On a bad day, they might be the recipient of all four. What's more, if you resided in one of the tenements down near the Harlem River, you could factor in the decaying stench from the bloated dead rats that floated in the flooded cellars.

Lancaster's adoring mother died unexpectedly of a cerebral hemorrhage when Burt was still in high school. Upon graduation, the troubled young man was offered an athletic scholarship to NYU, but soon dropped out.

At age 19, Lancaster met Nick Cravat, and not long after, they ran away to join the circus—the Kay Brothers Circus.

AUTHOR'S NOTE: As a little boy, I remember going to see the movie *Trapeze* with my parents and brother. We were vacationing up in Fish Creek, Wisconsin, that's in Door County. Lancaster starred opposite Tony Curtis, who had been a circus performer, as well.

During WWII, Lancaster served as an entertainment specialist in Italy. After the war, a talent agent spotted him in an elevator in New York City.

Famed Hollywood producer Hal B. Wallis discovered Lancaster took him under his wing, nurtured him and cast him in *The Rose Tattoo*. Lancaster spent nearly a month in Key West during the filming.

AUTHOR'S THROWBACK NOTE: When I was a student at UCLA, I somehow secured a job mentoring "misguided rich kids" out in the exclusive Palos Verdes peninsula of L.A. I worked with a young lady by the name of Bette Kovacs, whose father was the comedian Ernie Kovacs. At UCLA, we often had the sons or daughters of celebrities peppering our classes.

One evening, Bette invited me to a party. She said it was a "50's party" and we were to dress up accordingly. I had a pair of black & white saddle shoes, so I was off to a good start. I picked Bette up in Hollywood and we drove down Sunset Boulevard and swept up into the foothills of the Santa Monica Mountains and entered the ritzy enclave of Bel-Air, "Home to the Stars."

"My sister is married to this guy and his dad lives up here," Bette informed me, as we entered an impressive compound.

I couldn't believe my eyes. Outback of the expansive manse was a vast set of gymnastic rings and horizontal bars and weights.

"Jeez Louise, who's your sister's father-in-law?"

"Burt Lancaster."

Well, I don't remember much about that night back in the 70s, other than Burt wasn't in situ that night, but his Oscar for Best Actor in *Elmer Gantry* was right there on the mantle above the fireplace.

Now get this: Bette Kovacs and I would go our separate ways, and I would befriend a young coed at UCLA by the name of Deborah Zoe Dawson. Debbie and I became really good friends. We didn't date, just hung out. We would drive up to San Francisco on a whim or down to La Jolla to visit her parents. Debbie played the guitar and sang. When I graduated from UCLA, I left for an extended stay in Europe. Debbie Dawson formed a singing duet with none other than Bette Kovacs. Years later, after running around the world doing glamorous menial jobs and living in London working for Pan Am, I got a job running an acting school in Hollywood. I didn't have any money, so I slept in the acting studio (on the set). Eventually, I tried to make something of myself and I had the opportunity to write for the TV series *Trapper John, M.D.*, I met with the producers, and yes, you got it: one of the producers was Deborah Zoe Dawson.

Life's like that sometimes.

* * *

Here's a great photo of Burt Lancaster, Anna Magnani and Tennessee Williams at the Key West location for *The Rose Tattoo*:

https://www.wlrn.org/post/rose-tattoo-house-reborn-key-west

Did you look at the photo? You can also scroll down and have a peep at the trailer for *The Rose Tattoo*. It's just there below the photo.

It's dated, but powerful, and you get the odd glimpse of Key West.

CHAPTER 31—Truman Capote

Truman Capote was born Truman Streckfus Persons, September 30, 1924, in New Orleans.

In 1933, he moved to New York City to live with his mother (a former Miss Alabama) and her second husband, the handsome, virile José García Capote, a successful textile broker from the island of La Palma, in the Canary Islands. His stepfather embraced young Truman as a son and renamed him Truman García Capote.

**AUTHOR'S NOTE: On occasion, Gabrielle and I have holidayed in the Canary Islands. We stay on the island of Tenerife, in the verdant north, and not far Los Rodeos Airport the scene of the 1977 Pan Am KLM disaster. From the *finca* we stay in, high above the town of Puerto de la Cruz on the north coast, we can look off a short distance and see the neighboring island of La Palma. A patently glorious sight when the sun sets behind it and backlights the mountainous terrain.

As a young man, Truman Capote discovered Key West and used to chill with Tennessee Williams and Gore Vidal at South Beach or Higgs Beach.

They would go there to swim.

And cruise.

Eventually Truman Capote and Tennessee Williams and Gore Vidal would have a falling out. Each was jealous of the other's success, when their respected careers flagged or went in the toilet.

Indeed, Tennessee Williams ended up hating Capote and he loved rubbing Capote's nose in it, because at just a smidge (yes, a *smidge*) over 5-feet 4-inches, Tennessee veritably towered over Truman Capote who was an impish 5-feet-2 and one-half inches.

But once upon a time they had been amigos and Tennessee told this story about Truman Capote: "Truman had flown to Key West from Mexico, where he was to stay with Mrs. (Lee) Radziwill (younger sister of Jackie Kennedy) but left in a hurry because the mosquitoes were terrible. So he came to Key West from the Yucatan."

**WTF NOTE: As if we don't have the voracious little biting pests here?

"Capote had never been on the island before, and I suspect that he never will be here again. He was robbed the first night, losing all his credit cards, his address book, and about two thousand dollars. He said that he wasn't in his hotel room when the robbery occurred, but the police found no evidence of forced entry. I think he was cleaned out by some street boy he invited home for a private session!

"Truman came to Key West because he sold excerpts of his book *Answered Prayers* to *Esquire* magazine, and he made one of the conditions of the contract that the editor of the magazine, Don Erickson, had to fly to Key West to pick up the manuscript. He did that because Hemingway used to make Arnold Gingrich, the editor/founder of *Esquire* come to Key West to edit his stories before they were published. Truman was not about to get one thing less than Hemingway.

"One night Truman, Jimmy Kirkwood, and a friend of Truman's, I, and some other men went to dinner. Truman's friend was very drunk. The restaurant was full of tourists in double-knit suits, and since it was quite late, most of them were as tipsy as Truman's boyfriend. Some distance away, at a round table, sat three couples. Truman noticed them staring at us, and he said, 'Watch out! They'll be coming over for autographs!' And a few minutes later, one of the women at the table got up and came over, carrying a menu. She asked Truman to autograph the menu. He did. She left, and a few minutes later her husband came to our table and glared at Truman.

"'Are you Truman Capote?' And Truman said, 'I was this morning!' And the man unzipped his pants, and pulled out his cock. He said, holding it in the palm of his hand, 'Can you put your signature on this?' And Truman looked down at the cock, and up again, and he said. 'I don't know about my signature. But I can initial it!'"

* * *

In spite of everything going wrong on his visit to Key West, Capote made the Pier House Motel his winter home and wrote much of his unfinished manuscript for *Answered Prayers* here.

As I noted above, Truman Capote was also a patient of "Dr. Feelgood," and he had this to say of his addictive injections: "Instant euphoria. You feel like Superman. You're flying. Ideas come at the speed of light. You go 72 hours straight without so much as a coffee break. If it's sex you're after, you go all night."

Truman Capote died at the home of his old friend Joanne Carson, ex-wife of late-night TV host Johnny Carson, at noon on 25 August, 1984.

Capote had been a frequent guest on Johnny Carson.

Cause of death: "liver disease complicated by phlebitis and multiple drug intoxication."

Ex-friend Gore Vidal responded to news of Capote's death by calling it "a wise career move."

CHAPTER 32—Gore Vidal

Does Vidal have a love child in Key West?

"Possibly," Vidal said, in this interview from the newspaper *The Independent*.

The interviewer then asked: "There are rumours that you have a daughter from a relationship with a woman living in Key West, Florida, in the 1950s; are they true?"

"Possibly. I don't believe so. The father was either me or a German photographer. I believe the mother is dead. The child was a girl. Every Christmas, I would receive a picture of them all around the tree, and there's the little girl, looking like me. I could have a daughter, yes."

"Have you tried to contact her?"

"No. Why would I?"

"Because you might have a sense of responsibility, which, in the age of DNA…"

"I sent her mother money for an abortion. Which she used to go to Detroit, where she found a rich man."

**AUTHOR'S NOTE: Oh, boy…

Gore Vidal and Tennessee Williams were once bosom buddies, hanging out in Key West, carousing, as you now know. Vidal recalls one incident when he listened patiently as Tennessee Williams confessed to him his serial woes describing a long period on drugs, booze, insomnia and conversion to Catholicism, and said: "I slept through the 60s."

And Vidal responded, "You didn't miss anything."

Responding to the subject of the worldwide success of his old mates Tennessee Williams and Truman Capote, Vidal said this: "Whenever a friend succeeds, a little something in me dies."

CHAPTER 33—Leonard Bernstein

Bernstein was drawn to Key West so he could pursue a side of his sexuality that was not necessarily taboo back in New York, but frowned upon by, among others, his suspecting wife and disillusioned three children.

Bernstein first came to Key West in 1941, at the age of 23, lured by Tennessee Williams.

If you would like to see where the famous composer stayed upon arrival, jump on your bike and pedal up Duval until you arrive at the Southernmost House. Okay, stop in the shade in front of the main gate and look up at the house through those two towering palms which guard the gate. See the little gabled window up there on the right side? That's an attic, and that's where Leonard Bernstein spent his first nights.

Must have been stuffy and hot.

In a book released in October 2013, *The Leonard Bernstein Letters*, his wife reveals his homosexuality. Felicia writes: "You are a homosexual and may never change—you don't admit to the possibility of a double life, but if your peace of mind, your health, your whole nervous system depend on a certain sexual pattern, what can you do?"

Shirley Rhoades Perle, a friend of Bernstein, said that she thought Bernstein "required men sexually and women emotionally."

While in Key West, Bernstein started composing music for a ballet he called "Conch Town." The ballet itself never came to fruition, but Bernstein re-used selections from that score in two later works, the ballet "Fancy Free" and—are you sitting down?—a hit Broadway musical you just may have heard of called: *West Side Story*.

In later years, Bernstein was a frequent house guest of David Wolkowsky out on Ballast Key.

Bernstein died in 1990, at his Manhattan apartment The Dakota, a German Renaissance character building at 72nd and Central Park West.

The Dakota was where John Lennon was living when he was gunned down in the building's main entrance archway in 1980.

CHAPTER 34—Elizabeth Bishop

One of America's most brilliant poets and short story writers, an alcoholic and a lesbian, she arrived in Key West in the 1930s and first rented a flat at 529 Whitehead Street. Then in 1938, she had had sufficient success to be able to buy a clapboard eyebrow house at 624 White Street. She lived here until 1946, eventually moving over to an apartment at 611 Francis.

Bishop was friends with Tennessee Williams.

Elizabeth Bishop often drank herself into a stupor, starting "the hour before dawn" and sometimes continuing even until she was hospitalized. Which is a helluva binge, I'm thinking.

Her lover of more than a decade was a Brazilian self-taught landscape designer by the name of Lota de Macedo Soares. Soares overdosed after a mental breakdown brought on by Elizabeth Bishop's alcohol abuse, drug abuse and infidelity.

**AUTHOR'S CLINCAL NOTE: Yeah, that would do it.

CHAPTER 35—Judy Blume

Bestselling Children and YA author Blume lives part of the year in Key West with her husband George Cooper.

Blume serves on the board of the Key West Literary Seminar.

Her books have sold more than 85 million copies in 32 languages.

CHAPTER 36—Meg Cabot

Successful authoress of *The Princess Diaries* (and much, much more), Meg Cabot was advised to quit New York City by her account and escape to someplace with lower taxes.

Good advice…at the time.

Key West beckoned with its funky feel and historic Old Town, you see, Meg Cabot also needed to live somewhere where she didn't need a car—she doesn't drive.

But she does ride a bicycle.

CHAPTER 37—The Spice Girls

Was it Mel B's idea to visit Key West in the 1990s? Was she in the hunt for some same-sex strange, the randy little vixen?

The scantily clad Spice Girls pranced and tittered out to the Sunset Bar past Gabrielle and me when Gabrielle was standing at her easel painting. Noisy, attention seeking, snobbish…and that was just Pouty Posh.

The others were bearable.

As of this writing, the Spice Girls have just concluded a comeback tour in the UK.

Woohoo!

Except Pouty Posh, of course.

Aren't we the lucky ones.

ON AN ALLIED WTF NOTE: This doesn't have anything to do with Key West, but I just HAVE TO TELL YOU ABOUT IT.

I have to tell someone.

Yikes. Pour yourself a drink.

It won't be pretty.

A stunningly attractive and well-built German female model, who was employed as a nanny by the *America's Got Talent* judge, claims she had threesomes with Mel B and Mel B's husband over a period of seven years.

This all gets worse, so if you are easily offended, look away now.

Mel B does not dispute that she had a sexual relationship with the nanny (this is NOT good parenting, I'm thinking) and, what's more, felt the "deal she had struck" with the nanny was broken, because the nanny and Mel B's husband had sex "all by themselves" and didn't include her in all the fun.

The nanny went on to say that Mel B often acted as the

"cameraman" when they shot video of them having a threesome. This makes sense to me, as Scary Spice does have a background in TV.

You see, the nanny also claims: "My sexual and employment relationship with Melanie continued for approximately seven years until September 2016.

"During my time with Melanie, she and I had sex sporadically, sometimes having sex multiple times in a week.

"On the other hand (unfortunate choice of words), I never had any sexual relations with Stephen (the husband) without Melanie's instruction and without Melanie's actual or apparent consent.

"The only times Stephen and I had sex was when Melanie instructed Stephen and I to do so. Or when Melanie herself invited her husband to join us in the bedroom, at which point Melanie would often serve as the "cameraman" (**we know that already, get on with it) and record the sexual encounter or take part in the ménage a trois herself."

AUTHOR'S NOTE: Have I been living under a rock (or a chunk of coral) my whole life?

CHAPTER 38—Nick Carter

The choirboy-esque member of the Backstreet Boys was arrested and charged with battery on 13 January 2016 after he and a male friend battered two bartenders and a manager at the Hog's Breath Saloon (in Key West's Old Town) who refused to serve them (Carter and his incoherent cohort were legless).

In the police report, Carter's occupation was given as "none," which is exactly what he'll have if this sort of irresponsible behavior continues.

Which, from his dubious track record, will no doubt continue, indeed.

Eyeball this from the *Miami Herald*: "Key West police officer Daniel Blanco wrote in a report that General Manager Art Levin saw Carter and Papayans walk into the bar at 400 Front St. 'heavily intoxicated' and that bartender Mark Hanna refused to serve them because of that. The two defendants 'became agitated and aggressive' and were told to leave multiple times.

"They refused and were forced out of the bar by security. Once outside, Carter allegedly grabbed bartender Skylar Carden by the neck and punched him and Papayans reportedly head-butted Manager Matthew Stecher."

**FY-freaking-I: Carter and his family, including younger brother and fellow singer Aaron, used to live in an ocean-side compound across from Florida Keys Marathon International Airport. While living there, the family had brushes with authorities.

On May, 29, 2001, Carter ran his 45-foot Sea Ray aground in Knight Key Channel near the Seven Mile Bridge. Federal authorities said 3,762 square feet of seagrass was damaged. The following year, Carter paid a fine of $30,573 to finance restoration of the grass bed.

A sister, Bobbie Jean, who said she was a hairstylist, was arrested on Oct. 31, 2002, on a misdemeanor battery charge stemming from a fight in Marathon. On Nov. 6, 2003, she was arrested in Marathon for drunk driving (not the first time she was arrested for DUI).

**AUTHOR'S CAN'T WAIT NOTE: The Backstreet Boys are purportedly planning a tour with the Spice Girls.

CHAPTER 39—Bob Marley

A once-upon-a-time denizen of Key West's Chart Room Bar, Marley found solace and inspiration on the island.

Robert Nesta Marley, OM, was born on the 6th of February, 1945, in Nine Mile, Jamaica.

FY-IRIE-I: That "OM" up there after Bob Marley's name stands for "The Order of Merit," which is part of the Jamaican honors system. It is the fourth-highest honor that can be awarded by Jamaica.

You may remember that there was an assassination attempt on Marley in December 1976 in Jamaica, two days before he was due to headline a free concert organized by the then Jamaican Prime Minister in an effort to ease tension between two warring political groups.

Marley was shot, as was his wife and manager, at Marley's home. All survived. Despite significant injuries, Marley performed in front of 80,000 delirious fans. When asked why he showed up, Marley responded, "The people who are trying to make this world worse aren't taking a day off. How can I?"

In 1977, Marley was diagnosed with a malignant melanoma under a toe nail. Doctors sought to amputate the toe. Marley refused stating it was against Rastafarian.

The cancer spread to his lungs and brain, and Marley died from acral lentiginous melanoma at Miami Cedars of Lebanon Hospital (now called University of Miami Hospital). on 11 May 1981.

The King of Reggae was 36 years young.

The Green Parrot, on the corner of Whitehead and Southard, has frequently hosted a Bob Marley birthday tribute.

Ends up being a powerful and emotional evening.

CHAPTER 40—Jim Croce

Born in South Philly, Italian-American singer-songwriter Jim Croce was known for his hit songs in the early to mid-seventies: "Bad, Bad Leroy Brown," "Time in a Bottle," "You Don't Mess Around with Jim," "Operator," "Workin' at the Car Wash Blues," and "I Got a Name."

CHECK OUT: Jim Croce singing "I Got a Name," it just doesn't get any better than this: https://www.youtube.com/watch?v=YcqauC49Xmc

On Thursday, Sept. 20, 1973, Croce performed at Northwestern State College, 75 miles southeast of Shreveport, the day before his single "I Got a Name" was released.

About an hour after the concert ended, Croce and five others, including: second guitarist, Maury Meuhleisen; comedian George Stevens, who had opened the show, and the pilot Robert Elliott, took off from Natchitoches Regional Airport on their way to another concert in Sherman, Texas. They never made it. The plane hit a pecan tree at the end of the runway, spun around and crashed.

Jim Croce was 30.

Jimmy Buffett said this: "My memories of Jim have not faded one bit from my memory, from the first time we met in Key West back in the early seventies (playing at the Chart Room), to the days I spent with him on the road, watching and learning as an opening act. He was simply a big influence on me and I won't forget him."

GOOD-GUY NOTE: Jim Croce was a gentleman and a kind soul. When he was just starting out, he had booked a show at a southern college, but he became ill and was forced to cancel. When he recovered, his career took off and fame and fortune came his way…but he never forgot all those students that he felt he had let down. So he did another concert, but he kept the ticket prices low just like they were when he wasn't famous and when nobody knew who he was.

A gentleman, indeed, and many have never forgotten that.

The untimely death of Jim Croce caught record execs at ABC/Dunhill by surprise. One of their shining stars was prematurely extinguished. What to do? Find a new, young singer of similar ilk to fill the void.

Wait!

Wasn't there a young singer on their books who wrote his own material and was compared to writers like Kris Kristofferson?

And hadn't he been a friend of Jim Croce's and had been inspired by him.

He ticked all the boxes.

And it was an honor for Jimmy Buffett to follow in the footsteps of his mentor.

CHAPTER 41—Kenny Chesney

Chesney loved Key West so much he purchased a house here…then he realized he loved Key West so much, he decided to sell the house…

**WHISPERED NOTE: Look out the back door of The Bull, across the street, two houses off Duval. Just there. See it? *That* house. That very IMPRESSIVE house. You didn't hear it from me.

Chesney reportedly paid 5.7 million big ones for the 7,000-square-foot, six-bedroom, eight-bath estate. (**EIGHT BATHS! Gabrielle and I have to take cockpit showers on our sailboat.)

In a statement released by his record label, Chesney said, "It's funny how you can be moving out before you even move in. I may have been naïve to think I could just go down to the Keys and disappear. I wanted to find a place where I could just be and thought I'd found it. But with all the buzz since we signed the papers, the last thing I want to do to some place I love as much as Key West is change the dynamics, especially for the locals who have been so good to me, so I'm stopping the insanity before it begins. The 'For Sale' sign is back up, and I'm just not going to be able to take possession of the house."

But not to worry, Chesney still sneaks down here to play for overflowing crowds at the Hog's Breath and Sloppy's.

And this is what makes Key West such a glorious Mecca for musicians. BIG NAMES continue to return to the island to play in front of intimate, delirious crowds, to show their appreciation and to relive a bit of the magic of the good ol' days and revel in the nostalgia of a bygone era.

When life was simpler.

Here's Kenny at Sloppy's in August of 2017:

https://www.youtube.com/watch?v=HhTF65o5v8Y

CHAPTER 42—Jerry Jeff Walker

Jerry Jeff Walker (née Ronald Clyde Crosby) arrived in this world in 1942.

He didn't change his name until 1966.

If it hadn't been for Jerry Jeff Walker, there might have been no Jimmy Buffett as we now know.

JB's career was going in the toilet in Nashville in 1971, so he fled to the warmer climes of Miami and his old friend from Nashville Jerry Jeff Walker.

Walker had a mega hit with his "Mr. Bojangles" three years earlier and was living in impressive digs in Coconut Grove with his girlfriend Teresa "Murphy" Clark and her young son, Justin.

Jerry Jeff quickly did a diagnosis on his down-in–the-mouth friend and knew exactly what Jimmy needed—a ROAD TRIP!

Murphy read Jerry Jeff's mind and shouted: "Hell, Jerry Jeff, let's go to Key West!"

Walker agreed with Murphy and banged on and on about going down the Overseas Highway to Key West, and said: "There was a pot of gold at the end of the rainbow."

Turned out to just be pot for JB at the start.

The four of them jumped in Walker's classic 1947 silver-and-maroon Packard Deluxe Clipper Touring Sedan christened "The Flying Lady" and headed south.

To give you an idea what a monster these wheels were like, have a squizzy on this one of different livery, but similar vintage:

https://www.youtube.com/watch?v=I0wVmPQZTg0

Jimmy road shotgun, windows down, wind blasting his golden locks the 156 miles all the way to the rock and they were getting almost 11 miles-per-gallon and that was really good news.

BTW: Gasoline was round about $.35 to the gallon at the time.

Buffett was entranced by the Tanqueray clear waters of the

Keys, the floral fragrances, the feeling of having just taken a step back in time and his mood slowly brightened. When the gang arrived in Key West, they parked the 18-feet of gleaming metal at the foot of Duval, went into the Chart Room Bar at the Pier House Motel and a tall handsome bartender by the name of Tom Corcoran said (as you now know): "Welcome to Key West?" and offered JB a Heineken on the house and a broad smile.

Many of you are also aware of the story, but I believe it's worth revisiting to tip hats to Jerry Jeff Walker and Tom Corcoran.

Buffett had been too country for New York and too country for L.A., and not country enough for Nashville.

Key West turned out to be place where he could be himself.

**MUSICAL, ah, NOTE: Jerry Jeff Walker and Buffett co-wrote the song "Railroad Lady" on the last run of the old Pan-American Flyer from New Orleans to Nashville.

Have a listen to Walker and Buffett performing "Railroad Lady" in 1991: https://www.youtube.com/watch?v=5-kiPZ3SDSU

CHAPTER 43—Frank Gifford and Curt Gowdy

You may recall that Frank Gifford was a former sportscaster on ABC's *Monday Night Football*, pro football halfback and flanker for the New York Giants, husband of Kathie Lee Gifford, and serial adulterer. According to Johnny Carson's former lawyer, Henry Bushkin, Gifford had an affair with Carson's second wife Joanne in 1970.

Curt Gowdy was the beloved "voice" of the Boston Red Sox and a popular sportscaster for NBC and ABC.

In the 1980s, Gifford and Gowdy invested into the Oceanside Marina on Stock Island, now called the King's Pointe Marina, which was built in the 1960s by Tex Schramm and Clint Murchison, Jr., of the Dallas Cowboys.

Boo.

CHAPTER 44—The Beach Boys

The Beach Boys played at the Sunset Green. Do you know what that is? It's a newly opened (2018) "events lawn" which splits The Gates Hotel from the 24 Degrees North Hotel, out on North Roosevelt Boulevard.

The Green was mobbed with 1200 folk sandwiched in.

A few toddlers under the age of two.

Not sure why.

* * *

BEACHY NOTE: Did you know Glenn Campbell was in The Beach Boys?

I didn't.

Campbell played guitar on The Beach Boys' "Pet Sounds" album, and joined the band when Brian Wilson had his breakdown. Campbell toured with the band from December of 1964 until March of 1965, played bass and sang falsetto harmonies.

Here for your beachy enjoyment is a short interview with The Beach Boys and Glen Campbell:

https://www.youtube.com/watch?v=9KWXFqTgXf0

CHAPTER 45—Michael McDonald

You can't mistake that voice, can you?

Gritty.

Raspy.

Soulful.

Distinctive.

Michael McDonald's voice elicits a visceral response deep down inside of us.

He's been nominated for 10 Grammys and won *FIVE TIMES*.

He was with Steely Dan in the early '70s, became a Doobie Brother in the mid-'80s, and we get to see him in an intimate setting when he comes to Key West.

Look for Michael McDonald at the Sunset Green out on North Roosevelt Boulevard.

Get a babysitter for the toddlers.

**ANOTHER CELLULOID NOTE: Michael McDonald had huge success with the single "Sweet Freedom," which appeared on the soundtrack to the Billy Crystal and Gregory Hines film *Running Scared*.

Here he is singing it, along with some great clips from the Key West movie, plus Billy Crystal and Gregory Hines clowning around with him: https://www.youtube.com/watch?v=U-xetxYwyak

"Sweet Freedom" won the Golden Globe for Best Original Song, and McDonald won the Grammy for Best Male Pop Vocal Performance.

CHAPTER 46—The Tennessee Williams Theatre

The TWT gets its own entry on account of the litany of great artists they bring in.

The Tennessee Williams Theatre is located in the Tennessee Williams Fine Arts Center on the campus of the Florida Keys Community College on Stock Island (that's the neighboring island for those of you who haven't made it this far south yet—unlike Billy Crystal and Gregory Hines).

Over the years, the TWT has presented Art Garfunkel...Wynonna Judd and the Big Noise...Clint Black...Lyle Lovett with Vince Gill...The Temptations...The Four Tops...even Chubby Checker.

Dick Clark once said, "The three most important things that ever happened in the music industry are Elvis Presley, the Beatles and Chubby Checker."

Perhaps a fourth is The Tennessee Williams Theatre.

Perhaps.

CHAPTER 47—George Strait

George Strait is often down here on the rock, playing or recording at Jimmy Buffett's Shrimpboat Sound Studio.

If you go to the website for Shrimpboat Sound Studio, you will note right off that they don't list an address.

They don't want anybody to know.

Doesn't really matter, as everyone down here knows where it is anyway. If you make your way to the Key West Historic Bight, you are warm. If you aim for the Conch Seafood Restaurant, you are warmer. If you look for the white flat-roofed building with the security eye on top of the tall pole…just there along the boardwalk…you are HOT!

Did you hear about that George Strait story in *The New Yorker* magazine? Every time he went out in public, he wore his signature black cowboy hat. And everyone recognized him. They wouldn't leave him alone. They bugged him for his autograph. And he wasn't a happy-camper.

What to do?

He had to come up with some sort of disguise.

And then he had it. It hit him like a thunderbolt or possibly an ex who lived in Texas.

He came out in public WITHOUT his trademark cowboy hat.

Simple.

Clever even.

So now he's down here in Key West, and he's recording at Jimmy Buffett's Shrimpboat Sound Studio. And he's right in there playing and singing and wearing his hat.

When it was time to take a break and kickback for a few minutes, he employed stealth and went into his disguise.

He removed his hat.

A few minutes later, he was sitting outside, shirt off,

sunning himself, chilling.

And then a woman came right up to the "King of Country Music," gave him a good-hard look, and said these words: "My husband told me George Strait was in there recording. That can't be true. Why would he cut a record in this little place?"

"Honey," George Strait responded in his southern drawl, "I was just in there, and I didn't see him."

Best damn disguise ever.

CHAPTER 48—Major Orestes Lorenzo Perez

Major Perez was a handsome 36-year-old Cuban Air Force combat pilot, who had defected with an appropriated MiG fighter, and chose Key West as his safe haven.

For those who haven't read my first book in the KEY WEST Series, here is an encapsulated version of events:

Gabrielle and I were standing on the beach at Ft. Zach talking to Shark Man one day, when a Cuban MiG came in low across the water from the south and scorched the beach at Fort Zach just above tree height. The MiG turned, made another scorching pass nearly blowing our eardrums out, and landed at the nearby Naval Air Station Key West on Boca Chica Key.

Major Perez had believed that the Cuban government would be so embarrassed by his defection (and fly-by antics), they would allow his wife and family to leave, happy to see their backs. But it was not to be. Over the nearly two years the Major was separated from his wife, Victoria, who was a respected dentist, and his two young sons, the wife was lied to and told at various times that her husband was a traitor, planning to marry a rich American woman, was a homosexual, and even that he was dead.

Eventually, she lost her job and the government repossessed her home.

Back in America, the Major tried every possible avenue to get his family released and brought over to America. Helped financially by cousins in the U.S. and by the Valladares Foundation, a Northern Virginia-based human rights group, the Major lobbied Congress and President Bush (#41) who, during a campaign speech in Miami, urged Fidel Castro to let the family leave Cuba. When this didn't work, the Major resorted to a week-long hunger strike. It brought attention to his plight, but not success.

And then the story took a turn for the strange as life intervened: The Major was able to place a secret phone call to Havana, through Canada. He actually got his wife on the phone. After she spoke for a few minutes, she passed the phone to their little son, 6-year-old Alejandro, and Alejandro said these words: "Daddy, you are a pilot, come get us in a helicopter. Fly over the house and drop down a ladder."

And from little Alejandro, the Major had his inspiration.

The first thing he had to do was learn how to fly. *What! He's the Cuban equivalent of Top Gun!* Well, it's this way: He had to obtain a US pilot's license, but language was not the problem, technology was. He may have been able to fly a sophisticated MiG-23 jet fighter, but he had to take lessons to learn how to fly a simple twin-engine Cessna. This is sort of like asking a teenager, who can hack into the Pentagon, to do simple math in his head.

Then he had to find a plane. He didn't want to rent one. He feared that if he were shot down on his flight to Cuba, authorities would think he had just wanted to steal the plane to return to Cuba. Eventually, Valladares co-chairwoman Elena Diaz-Verson Amos, a wealthy Cuban-born widow, heard of the Major and his family and she put up $30,000 of her own money to buy an aircraft.

The plan: His wife was to pretend as if she were taking the two boys to the beach for a seaside outing. The Major would take off from Marathon, fly the 107 miles to Veradero, Cuba, at an altitude of **six feet**—and under US and Cuban radar—then he would set the twin-engine Cessna down on the congested Veradero highway, just yards from where his wife and sons would be "enjoying a day at the beach" and his wife and two boys would run for their lives.

From his days with the Cuban military, he knew he had a 40-second window before he would be targeted by missiles.

The Major would eventually tell friends in America: "Even I thought the plan was crazy, but I had to try. I would rather die than leave my family there."

The Major smuggled the details of his plan in a letter hand-delivered by two female Mexican human rights activists. When his wife received the letter, she knew it was the real deal and not some government ruse—the Major had addressed his beloved wife by his pet name for her "Cuchita."

The two human rights activists also accompanied the Major's wife on a reconnaissance visit to the pickup site to do a mock run-through. Then they purchased international-orange shirts and hats for her and the boys, so the Major could spot them quickly upon touching down.

The entire preparation took nine months.

On the night before the mission, the Major was praying at a chapel. "This sister came to me and said, 'Don't be afraid. Your long trip will be a success.' How could she know about my plans? I believed that God was speaking to me then and that God would be with me."

The Major roared down the runway in Marathon in his twin-engine Cessna at 5:05 the next afternoon and stayed low over the aquamarine waters of the Florida Straits. He hugged the ocean and prayed that his plane would not be intercepted.

The Major's wife was watching as a dark speck skimmed the waters of northern Cuba and then fought to land just over a bus, avoid a street sign, and then a boulder in the middle of the road.

The Major's wife screamed to her children: "Run! Run! It's Daddy!"

And the 40 seconds began.

Tick. Tick. Tick.

The Major braked desperately to avoid hitting an approaching truck, which screeched to a halt and only just avoided hitting the propellers. The Major would later say he would never forget the bug-eyed look on the stunned truck driver's face.

Tick. Tick. Tick.

The Major had to turn the plane around in front of startled onlookers. Cars in the way pulled over and made a path out.

Tick. Tick. Tick.

His wife and children threw open the door and burst into the airplane. The boys were crying and hugging their daddy, forgetting that there wasn't time for that.

Tick. Tick. Tick.

Looking back on that day, the Major says the hardest part, was when his wife and kids jumped into the plane—and he didn't even have time to touch them. "They were crying. I had to say to the children, 'Shut up and sit down.' I had to fly the plane."

Tick. Tick. Tick.

With more rubberneckers stacking up, the Major roared down the Veradero Highway, nearly clipped a wing on a car, lifted the nose of the twin-engine Cessna and once again hugged the waves as the sun set in the west.

Twenty-one minutes and 43 seconds later, they were out of missile range and entered U.S. airspace. "We did it!" the Major shouted triumphantly. "We did it!"

Still gives me goose bumps.

Safe on American soil, the Major will tell you: "I wake up every night at 4 a.m. I look at my wife. I kiss my sons. I watch them sleep. I cannot believe that they are here with me."

And his wife, Victoria, will add: "I knew he would come, I always knew it. I believe in him. I believe in love."

And perhaps most of us don't even know how lucky we are.

CHAPTER 49—The Blue Paper

They NEED OUR SUPPORT.

Check this out:

For nearly six years *The Blue Paper* has "been giving us the OTHER SIDE of the story."

The Blue Paper is the Key West version of Woodward and Bernstein.

Naja Girard does the research.

Amber Nolan investigates.

Arnaud Girard creates the eye-opening video documentaries and draws the in-your-face, poignant, local political cartoons.

This team, along with a few professional pit-bull stringers, sniff, dig, and unearth political, environmental and legal smoke and mirrors and aren't afraid to open a seething can of worms. They get the story and tell it with a loud voice.

If they didn't tell the story, the story would never be told.

In other words, THE TRUTH, not what politicians want you to believe, not what law enforcement want you to believe, not what developers want you to believe, and not what other news media outlets want you to believe.

THE TRUTH.

The Blue Paper fights corruption, exposes inside players, and gives a voice to the little people, the you-and-me people, so that we are not ignored, forgotten and tread on.

Okay, Dear Reader, please listen up: During nearly six years of in-depth investigative reporting, NO ONE HAS BEEN PAID.

You heard right. *No one.*

They do it because they believe in it.

They do it because it needs to be done.

They do it for *us.*

That being said, go online, read the great stories, watch the videos, pay attention to the political cartoons.

Let your eyes be opened, take it in, do some hard thinking.

And think about supporting *The Blue Paper*.

They can't go on without our support.

And remember: If *The Blue Paper* didn't exist, Wisteria Island (Christmas Tree Island) just might not exist in its glorious present form either.

Be an email subscriber: **thebluepaper.com**

Follow them on Facebook at Key West The Newspaper (The Blue Paper).

Pass it on, *por favor*.

CHAPTER 50—The Revivalists

The Revivalists were gigging at the Green Parrot and the Sunset Pier for many years before they made it.

Now they're big.

Huge.

But they came back to Key West and played here at the amphitheater (Truman Park) on 6 April.

And they still drank at the Parrot.

Have a peep at this on their "Key West Fans of The Revivalists FB page" back when they played the Green Parrot, back when they weren't as big as they are now:

https://www.facebook.com/KeyWestFansOfTheRevivalists/

The Conch Republic rocks!

CHAPTER 51—David Wolkowsky

David Wolkowsky was known as "Mr. Key West."

And the "man who built Key West."

For those of you who don't know the skinny on David Wolkowsky, let me just bring you up to speed by slapping this from *KEY WEST, Part II, the Seagull, I mean the Sequel*, down in front of you:

In 1963, Wolkowsky acquired a chunk of choice waterfront property near Mallory Square bearing the old Cuban Ferry Dock at the foot of Duval for $106,000. A princely sum in those days. He had designs on building a chic resort. Having said that, there was nothing about Key West in the early 60s that smacked of chic (although the Casa Marina did exude a certain Raffles elegance) and many locals scoffed at David Wolkowsky. They scoffed until he had the 1890 Porter Steamship office jacked up off its foundation, moved 300 feet out into the channel, set on pilings in 40 feet of water and renovated into the beckoning form of Tony's Fish Market.

Tony's was predominantly a restaurant and cocktail lounge where guests could get shit-faced while watching the shrimp boats slip past on their way in and out of the harbor.

Sounds like it would have been my kind of place.

**HAVE A PEEK at this great old black-and-white photograph of David Wolkowsky sitting in his vintage Rolls-Royce, out in front of Tony's Fish Market:
https://www.floridamemory.com/items/show/135719

Then in 1967, Wolkowsky constructed a motel around Tony's, which was called the Pier House Resort *Motel*, as I've alluded to. Then he added 50 rooms to the existing 50 rooms, and more additions and upgrades over the years, until the venue evolved into the Pier House Resort. With the "motel" label removed, it became a magnet for celebrities.

When writer Truman Capote appeared on the scene and desired to spend the winter, he asked Wolkowsky to show him the very best rooms in the hotel. After having a peek at the best units, Wolkowsky invited Capote over for a drink to his temporary residence: a 45-foot, two-bedroom, double-wide trailer, covered in bamboo and parked 10 feet from the hotel's fetching waterfront.

Capote like the view, craved the privacy, and begged Wolkowsky to rent him the trailer for the winter.

Wolkowsky agreed and moved into one of his own suites.

When a new watering hole was needed, Wolkowsky appropriated one of his larger hotel rooms and transformed it into the now world-famous Chart Room Bar.

And you know what's coming next, don't you?

When Jimmy Buffett turned up on the scene, Wolkowsky was taken with his friendly, affable manner, and agreed to let him play in the Chart Room for tips.

Later, for pay.

The next time you're down in Key West, have a wander over there to the Chart Room. Go when it's a sultry, steamy evening. The place absolutely oozes a feeling of an era gone by and there are many stories to be learned within its walls about its former denizens.

Now catch this: Not only was the Pier House Resort a turning point in backwater Key West's transformation from a mosquito-infested, mangrove-covered military outpost to an eclectic and vibrant tourist destination, but so was another Wolkowsky project, the original Reach Resort at the other end of Simonton (where Gabrielle once worked the front desk).

Over the years, David Wolkowsky renovated more than 100 derelict conch houses, two-story wooden structures, with shady verandas that were built in the 19th century, saving them from decay.

And you've heard about his "private island" out on Ballast Key, about 9 miles or so southwest of Mallory Square. If you stand on the pier at Mallory Square and gaze off past Sunset Key and Wisteria Island (Christmas Tree Island), way out there toward the setting sun lies Ballast Key. David Wolkowsky purchased this 24-acre, scrub-choked rock from the Navy in the late 1970s and built a beachside 4,000-square-foot mansion with eight bedrooms, lots of windows, lots of ceiling fans, a spiral staircase, a helipad, and its own desalination plant.

Check out just a few of the celebrities who paid a visit or spent the night out on Ballast Key: Richard Burton, Elizabeth Taylor, Rudolf Nureyev, Leonard Bernstein, Truman Capote, Tennessee Williams, Lillian Hellman, Gloria Estefan, Jimmy Buffett, British Prime Minister Edward Heath, Prince Michael of Greece, and the Bee Gees.

You've probably heard that the island even had a cameo appearance in the James Bond movie *Licence to Kill*, and the island and Wolkowsky made the pages of the novel as well. "David, it's James, James Bond…I've broken into your island. I hope you don't mind."

The above is impressive and awe-inspiring in its own right, but what I find even more impressive is David Wolkowsky's loyalty, his integrity and his passion.

In reference to Tennessee Williams: While others such as Capote and Vidal were falling out with Williams, David Wolkowsky maintained a lifelong relationship, and he had this to say, "I saw too many people come and go with Tennessee, so I kept a very pleasant and semi-formal relationship with him. I always saw the best side of him. Just because I never tried the other."

David Wolkowsky died at the age of 99, on September 23rd 2018.

He had a good run.

A great run, actually.

And his legacy will live on: Just before his death, he agreed to donate his island, his Ballast Key, which had been on the market for a salty 15.8 million.

The island was donated through a two-part transaction that gave it initially to The Nature Conservancy and then to the U.S. Fish and Wildlife Service. The two groups will co-manage the island "for marine and coastal research and education, while preserving its natural resources, including critical habitat for sea turtles, birds, butterflies and fish."

As of this writing, the U.S. Fish and Wildlife Service is working to change the name of the island from Ballast Key to "David Wolkowsky Key."

Cool.

**FIND A STREET NOTE: David Wolkowsky has a street in Key West named after him. Your assignment is to take a stroll and find the street WITHOUT Googling it.
HINT: It's a four-minute walk from The Bull.

CHAPTER 52—Richard Burton

Richard Burton was born Richard Jenkins, Jr., in a dank, stone house beneath an impressive stone viaduct in Pontrhydyfen, Glamorgan, Wales, on the 10ᵗʰ of November, 1925.

He was the twelfth of thirteen children to a coalminer father, and a weary barmaid mother who worked in a nearby pub called the Miner's Arms.

Burton's father was a "12-pint-a-day" man and would go off on drinking and gambling sprees for weeks on end, leaving his poor wife to look after the 13 offspring.

Smacks of *Angela's Ashes*, wouldn't you agree?

Richard Burton's mother died on Halloween, only six days after giving birth to her thirteenth child. Cause of death was purported to be from hygiene neglect and dust from the coal mines.

Richard was just two.

Richard's elder sister ended up raising him and he said his sister was more of a mother to him than his biological mother.

As an adult, and now a famous thespian, Richard Burton used to come to Key West to drink, hang out with David Wolkowsky, visit Ballast Key (as you now know)…but, more importantly, to see a certain *Philip* Burton, a man who he called "father."

Young Richard first met Philip Burton at the Port Talbot Secondary School (in Wales) where Philip Burton was teaching mathematics and history. He also taught drama and gave young Richard his first real exposure to the magical world that is theatre.

Philip Burton believed young Richard, 21 years his junior, to be the proverbial diamond in the rough, and with great potential, so he began to mentor him, tutor him, and direct him much like Professor Henry Higgins did with Eliza Doolittle in *Pygmalion* and *My Fair Lady*.

Young Richard often had his tutelage on the mountains overlooking the poor, working-class steel town of Port Talbot below, and later described the lessons as "sheer hell."

Philip was relentless and driven in his teaching of young Richard, enlightening him to all he knew about literature and drama and the great writers.

Philip even toned down and reconstructed young Richard's strong Welsh accent, as well, with rigorous elocution training, and developed young Richard's distinctive, deep baritone voice. These were the only formal voice lessons Richard Burton received and within 10 years they had taken him to Stratford-upon-Avon, the birthplace of William Shakespeare.

In autumn of 1943, Philip planned to adopt young Richard, but was not legally permitted to do so as Philip was 20 days too young. It was a legal requirement that the "adoptive parent" be at least 21 years older than his charge. Young Richard did become Philip's legal ward though, and changed his surname to "Richard Burton."

Philip Burton eventually emigrated to New York, to work in the theatre, and became a U.S. citizen.

Philip came to Key West in 1964, already a successful Broadway stage producer, writer, director and expert on Shakespeare, had a nose around, liked what he saw and started hunkering down here to avoid the harsh New York winters.

When he returned to Key West to live permanently, he contracted a local fellow by the name of Christian Alderson to find him a suitable home, and restore it. Anderson did just that, offering Philip the very home he had been living in at 608 Angela Street, which is just around the corner and up a few streets from where Gabrielle and I used to live in our dump at 404 Aronovitz Lane.

When Richard Burton had long found fame and would come to Key West with Elizabeth Taylor, the pair always stayed with his "father" at 608 Angela.

In his later years, Philip Burton became quite withdrawn, avoided going out, and was known as "The Hermit of Angela Street."

Here's a photo of a young Richard Burton with his adopted father Philip Burton during better years:

https://www.tivysideadvertiser.co.uk/leisure/whatson/156 00457.fluellen-theatre-company-to-stage-granton-street-at-theatr-gwaun/#gallery0

Of his surrogate father, Richard Burton said: "He was an impressive man of great intellect. I owe him everything."

Richard Burton was nominated for an Academy Award seven times, but never won an Oscar.

He drank three bottles of vodka a day and smoked up to five packs of cigarettes.

Richard Burton died at the age of 58 from a brain hemorrhage at his home in Geneva, Switzerland.

CHAPTER 53—James Leo Herlihy

You may not know the name, but you will most certainly know the name of the novel he penned: *Midnight Cowboy*.

James Leo Herlihy, novelist, playwright and actor, was a dear friend of Tennessee Williams and lived in Key West off and on from 1957 to 1973, most notably in the guest house at 709 Baker's Lane, up on Solares Hill at a nose-bleed height of 18 feet above sea level.

Tennessee Williams was Herlihy's mentor (until they fell out, drugs and alcohol will do that to you) and they both employed gritty, markedly taboo themes in their work. Together, they would go swimming over at South Beach or Higgs Beach pretty much every day, at twilight.

Herlihy said this about his partner in crime Tennessee Williams: "It was inexpressibly comforting to have the daily company of a kindred spirit; and just knowing we were involved in the same sort of lunatic pursuit provided some essential ground that meant everything to me."

Herlihy didn't write *Midnight Cowboy* when he was living in Key West though, then he drank, and did drugs.

The town excited me too much," Herlihy said. "I spent all my time exploring, walking the streets. The place was mysterious, funky, and indescribably exotic. It had much of the charm of a foreign country, but you had the post office and the A&P and the phone worked, so life was easy.

"Key West was still a pretty well-kept secret," he went on, "neither a tourist favorite nor a literary and cultural hotspot: Nightlife was delightful, totally unsophisticated, nonliterary."

Herlihy committed suicide at the age of 66, at his "Swish Alps" hillside home in the Silver Lake area of Los Angeles, by taking an overdose of stolen Phenobarbital pills.

CHAPTER 54—James Kirkwood

James Kirkwood was the co-author of the book for the hit Broadway and West End musical *A Chorus Line*, and the partner of James Leo Herlihy.

A Chorus Line earned him both a Tony and the 1976 Pulitzer Prize for Drama, one of the few musicals ever to receive this honor.

Kirkwood was born in L.A. in 1924, a "child of Hollywood" as the son of silent movie stars, the womanizing James Kirkwood, Sr., and the sultry Lila Lee who rose to millionaire-status fame and then crashed and burned like a dying meteorite before young James' teenage eyes.

For James Kirkwood's writing efforts on *A Chorus Line*, he received 1% of the gross—not such a great deal, one might think, but that 1% made him a millionaire.

Kirkwood first visited Key West in 1963. He purchased an old cigar-maker's cottage at 1117 Watson and resided there for ten years. (**Gabrielle and I stayed for a short time nearly right across the street at 1112 Watson with an Italian artist friend, Alberto, and his American wife, Joan.)

Here's what James Kirkwood had to say about Key West: "This is a crazy little island. It's not Florida, maybe not even America, but a country and state of mind. It's the end of the line, even the world."

And he went on: "Key West was always a swinging place. There was never a stigma attached to anything you did in your private life. Key West has always held a great attraction for people who are a little tiled, a little crazy. They're very eccentric, not your average, run-of-the-mill, middle-America type, but people a little off-center, even kinky."

James Kirkwood died in his Manhattan apartment of AIDS-related complications in 1989, aged 64.

CHAPTER 55—Robert Frost

Robert Frost, who served as U.S. poet laureate in 1958-59, first visited Key West in 1934 and wrote one of his best-known poems, "The Gift Outright," on the island.

**FY-stanza-I: A U.S. poet laureate is, simply said, the official poet of the US of A, whose task is to raise the national awareness of writing poetry, and, yes, the reading of poetry, as well. (I don't know about you, but I did not know that. I had to look it up.)

With a surname like "Frost," dear Robert just had to winter in Key West, which he did and enjoyed from 1945 to 1960.

I would now just say that Key West is never supposed to have a frost, but I won't because then you would roll your eyes at me.

Robert Frost stayed in a small cottage on the grounds of the home of local hostess and preservationist Jessie Porter. Porter's home and the cottage, which has been named a National Literary Landmark, still stand at 410 Caroline Street, right down the street from my "office" The Bull.

Where I do much of my thinking.

I mean drinking.

Robert Frost won the coveted Pulitzer Prize twice.

If you want to see what Robert Frost's cottage looks like today, have a squizzy at the listing from Airbnb, right here:

https://www.airbnb.co.uk/rooms/13989296?guests=1&adults=1&sl_alternate_dates_exclusion=true&source_impression_id=p3_1558529715_fnxbXX84Q3JBWgcq

CHAPTER 56—Jessie Porter

Jessie Porter was born in 1898, was a fifth-generation conch, and her lush tropical garden was often the center of Key West society, such as it was back then. As a hostess, she was Key West's answer to Gertrude Stein, and often held court in the garden when artists and writers came to boast, argue, drink and seduce.

Tallulah Bankhead, Tennessee Williams, Vincent Price, Gloria Swanson, Elizabeth Bishop, and a fan-dancer by the name of Sally Rand were often in attendance, during those steamy tropical soirées.

Here's a great photo of the siren Sally Rand visiting sailors at the Naval Hospital in Key West:
https://www.pinterest.com/pin/373376625349292293/

FYI: Sally Rand used to own a home at 916 Eisenhower Drive, in the meadows, distance from the Porter House, a good 25 minute walk away. If you have a bicycle you can do it in 8 minutes.

When we first arrived in Key West, Gabrielle worked at the Reach, as I mentioned above, then she found more amenable employment in the "garden" on the Duval side of the "Porter Mansion" (just there by the Porter House), selling artwork and cutting mats, then in the evenings, she would accompany me down to "Sunset" where we sold our Sunset Photos (in nice mats, might I add).

It was Miss Jessie who'd decided that the old Porter Mansion be painted emerald green to reflect the nearshore waters of Key West. Originally, the structure had been white, but Miss Jessie felt tourists visiting from the Great White North had seen enough of white during the winter and would appreciate the tropical colors.

Good thinking, say I.

Okay, for those of you up for a little island adventure, jump on your bike and pedal like hell over to the Key West cemetery and see if you can find Jessie Porter's grave.

CLUE: "Jessie Porter **Newton."

**HIT THE SKIDS NOTE: I don't know where else to put this in, so I'll just stick it in here: Tallulah Bankhead eventually went off the deep end and began taking dangerous cocktails of drugs to fall asleep. Things got so bad, her maid had to tape her arms down to prevent her from popping more pills lest she awake in a stupor. In her later years, Bankhead had serious accidents and several psychotic episodes from sleep deprivation and drug abuse. She hated being alone and her loneliness manifested as depression.

In 1956, playing the "truth game" with her dear friend Tennessee Williams, she said: "I'm fifty-four, and I wish always, always, for death. I've always wanted death. Nothing else do I want more."

CHAPTER 57—Ernest Hemingway

The iconic face of Key West.

The iconic image of machismo.

Boozer.

Boxer.

Lover.

Hunter.

Fisherman.

Everything has been written about Hemingway, much of it true and unembellished, so no need to prattle on and tell you what you already know.

That means I'm not going to write about:

The URINAL

Or the polydactyl CATS (although that adorable kitten by the vintage typewriter deserves a mention)

Or the SWIMMING POOL

Or the PENNY stuck in the cement of the swimming pool

Or the BOXING matches at what is now Blue Heaven

Or the MOB

Or FISHING the Gulfstream

Or about his FOUR wives

Or the INFIDELITY

Or about the *PILAR* (Was she a fifth wife?)

But, what I will write about is something that you might have known, but I've only just learned, Hemingway was an ABSINTHE aficionado.

Hemingway once said this: "Key West, it's the best place I've ever been, anytime, anywhere. Got tight last night on absinthe and did knife tricks. Great success shooting the knife underhand into the piano. The woodworms are so bad here and eat the hell out of all furniture that you can always claim the woodworms did it."

And he said this:

"It takes a man with hair on his chest to drink five absinthe and champagne cocktails and still handle the English language…"

As a diabetic, Papa took most of his drinks (including absinthe and double daiquiris) without sugar.

Good that he was so concerned about his blood sugar levels.

FY-alcohol 101-I: Did you know there was an adult beverage called the "Death in the Afternoon?"

It's a cocktail made up of absinthe and champagne invented by the man himself (think of the hours researching put into perfecting it).

If you feel the need to whip one up to nurse the woes you're experiencing while watching the playoffs or the golf or the speedboat races, here's the recipe: "Pour one jigger absinthe into a champagne glass. Add iced champagne until it attains the proper opalescent milky consistency. Drink three to five of these slowly."

Glad he said "drink…slowly."

AUTHOR'S WTF NOTE: Absinthe used to contain a psychoactive ingredient called thujone, which is a byproduct of wormwood.

When asked in an interview if rumors of him taking a pitcher of martinis to work every morning were true, Hemingway answered, "Jeezus Christ! Have you ever heard of anyone who drank while he worked? You're thinking of Faulkner. He does sometimes—and I can tell right in the middle of a page when he's had his first one. Besides, who in hell would mix more than one martini at a time?"

"Write drunk, edit sober," Hemingway has said, as well, and that seems more like it. Find me a picture where he doesn't have a drink in his hand. Okay, that one with the marlin, but find me another one.

And he said this about beer: "You have to work hard to deserve to drink it. But I would rather have a bottle of Ballantine

Ale than any other drink after fighting a really big fish. When something has been taken out of you by strenuous exercise Ballantine puts it back in. We keep it iced in the bait box with chunks of ice packed around it. And you ought to taste it on a hot day when you have worked a big marlin fast because there were sharks after him."

In April 1959, English theatre critic Kenneth Tynan was traveling to Cuba to interview Fidel Castro (who'd recently chased Batista off the island), and called in to see Tennessee Williams in Key West and asked the playwright if he would like to accompany him.

"I've arranged to have lunch with Hemingway at the Floridita tomorrow, "said Tynan, "Why not join us?"

"Hemingway?" Tennessee said. "You're joking, right? I've heard he kicks people like me in the crotch."

But he went.

Williams, who admired Hemingway's work, nevertheless was unnerved by the tall and bear-like novelist who greeted him and Tynan with crushing handshakes and, well, bear hugs as they walked into the famous Floridita bar and restaurant.

Hemingway ordered Papa Dobles (double frozen daiquiris) all round, signed a few autographs, and then had to listen to a trio of singers salute him with a new song they'd written about a local lesbian who could not, no matter how much she tried "…change her appetites to suit Papa."

Hemingway laughed and hugged the singers, tipping them well, before explaining to Williams that the bronze bust of himself on the bar in the corner was always covered up for Lent.

Williams then told Hemingway he'd met the bullfighter Ordóñez in Spain, describing him as "…a lovely boy, very friendly, very accessible." Hemingway said nothing. Williams then said:

"I was introduced to Pauline back in Key West. I was very sorry to hear of her death…"

"She died like everybody else," said Hemingway, "and after that she was dead."

Ernest Hemingway and Tennessee Williams—both now dead—are United States postage stamps.

CHAPTER 58—Martha Gellhorn

Key West.

Christmas, 1936.

Hemingway was sitting on his favorite barstool at the original Sloppy's (which is now Capt. Tony's), when the leggy blonde Martha Gellhorn sashayed in with her mother in tow.

Hemingway flirted.

Gellhorn flirted.

Gellhorn's mother watched on with amusement.

And it was the beginning of the end for Hemingway "wife number-two," Pauline.

Hemingway married Martha Gellhorn in 1940 just three weeks after his divorce to Pauline was finalized.

But Gellhorn grew to resent her fame as Hemingway's third wife, saying "that she had no intention of being a footnote in someone else's life."

She went on: "I've been a writer for over 40 years. I was a writer before I met him and I was a writer after I left him. Why should I be merely a footnote in his life?"

Gellhorn was considered one of the great war correspondents of the 20th century. She reported on every major world conflict that took place during her 60-year career.

Lacking official press credentials to witness the Normandy landings, she hid in a hospital ship's toilet, and upon landing impersonated a stretcher bearer.

She was the only woman to land on the Normandy beaches on D-Day, 6 June, 1944.

And she was among the first journalists to report from the death camps at Dachau after the concentration camp was liberated by American troops on 29 April, 1945.

All that, yet we know of her because she sat on a barstool next to Ernest Hemingway at Sloppy Joe's.

CHAPTER 59—Jackie Gleason

In 1964, during "The Golden Era" of American television, Gleason moved his top-rated show down to Miami Beach from New York. On one occasion, when his show was on hiatus, he snuck down to Key West, but didn't stay long. He missed his golf. Indeed he played nearly every day back up in Miami, but when he arrived in Key West, he found that the course out on Stock Island only had nine holes.

And awaaay we go!

Back up to Miami.

The Key West golf course was opened in 1924, but it wasn't until 1966 that it offered 18 holes.

CHAPTER 60—Jimmy Buffett

Like Hemingway, everything has been written about Buffett down here on the rock, such as singing for tips and tequila and blow at the Chart Room, hanging with Tom Corcoran, managing one of Capt. Tony's mayoral bids, wearing T-shirts at his concerts that ask that nagging question: "WHERE IS BUM FARTO?", the Broadway musical, and being a member in good standing of the naughty Key West Club Mandible, a roaming social club "dedicated to inebriation and fornication."

What I would like to address though is when Buffett and Jim Harrison made their documentary entitled *Tarpon*. You may know a bit of the story. Here it is in more detail. This as told by Buffett to *MEN'S JOURNAL,* shortly after the passing of his dear friend Jim Harrison:

"There are so many funny things we did that people never knew about. One time, we worked on this *Tarpon* movie together, a fishing documentary from the '70s. Basically, we had no fucking idea what we were doing at the time, starting with the script. [Director] Guy de la Valdene had all the money and sent a crew that was all French. I speak French now, but I didn't at the time, so there was a huge communication issue. So we're in the Keys and taking out boats with [poet] Richard Brautigan and [novelist] Tom McGuane. It really captured the Key West of the '70s. It's sort of a treasure today.

"But we didn't really get paid for it. I wrote the music and Harrison was going to do the narration. And so, they said they'd give us a ticket and we could live at Guy's family's house on the outskirts of Paris, and we'd work in town. So I told Guy, I said, 'Don't call me before you're down to, like, six hours of footage, because I really can't do anything until it's down to that.' When we arrive, the house looks like a castle or something out of a movie, with a boat and everything. Jim had to go in earlier than us to work on narration, and came back out to the castle in the afternoon and he went, 'Jesus Christ, you're not going to believe this.' And I said, 'What?' And he said, 'Well they got it wrong, they don't speak fucking English. They thought you said 60 hours!' And I went, 'What?!' He said, 'Yeah, Jimmy said call us when we're down to 60 hours.' And I went, 'Holy shit.'

"So we had nothing to do. Fortunately, we scored a bag of pot from somebody coming from Spain and had the key to the wine cellar. So we lived like gypsies in the palace for about three weeks before they madly got this thing down to where we could go in and work.

"We worked in the studio in the middle of Paris, there were just cubicles and everybody was working on different projects. There was this girl cutting another film and she'd come over, and she was loving the beauty of what we were shooting. And then I look at her stuff and I said, 'Jim, man, it's like a porno film or something!' He said 'What?!' and then he went back and started charming the girl, and it turns out it was the first *Emmanuelle*. So we were cutting a fish movie in one booth, and they were cutting *Emmanuelle* in the next booth. She would let us come back in and watch the movie. We said, 'Boy, this is going to be a lot better than our fish movie.'"

Okay, Dear Voyeur, I mean Reader, sink your teeth into the trailer for the "fish movie":

https://www.youtube.com/watch?v=TDy3N5whzII

CHAPTER 61—Rudolf Nureyev

In March of 1938, Nureyev was born on the speeding Trans-Siberian Express (his mother was traveling to see his father, a Red Army commissar).

In 1961, in Paris, Nureyev evaded KGB agents and successfully defected to the West.

In 1963, he starred with Margot Fonteyn in a Royal Ballet production in New York City. Sitting in the audience was Jackie Kennedy, who immediately became enraptured.

Nureyev soon quit New York and fled to Key West to escape the rumor mill and ensuing pursuit of paparazzi after his purported affair with not only Jackie Kennedy, but her sister Lee Radziwill, as well.

Nureyev came to Key West to fish, but not for tarpon, and he liked to boast that he was the "sexiest man alive" and simply "too good a lover not to share my body with others."

And share it he did.

Frequently.

He was only 54 when he died of complications from AIDS in 1993.

CHAPTER 62—Joe Cocker

Cocker gigged at the "Snake Pit" in the '70s.

The Snake Pit was the locals' affectionate *nom de guerre* given to the Old Anchor Inn at 208 Duval (now the Red Garter, right there by Rick's).

The Snake Pit was a dive.

It had manky restrooms that were always flooded and the owners had cleverly plopped down a "plank" of bricks, and you had to walk the plank so you could get to and from the pisser without getting your sandals wet, or end up knee deep in the poopla.

The owners Bud and Dorothy MacArthur were forced to erect a picket fence lining the sidewalk out front to accede to city demands as there had been a shitload of complaints of drunks falling out the front door.

This is sounding more and more like my kinda place.

Nary a night would pass when you'd stagger by and not hear Joe Cocker grinding out the Lennon/McCartney "She Came In Through The Bathroom Window."

If you want to have your knickers blown off, go to YouTube and listen to the Beatles' version…and then do the Joe Cocker version and get ready to hold on.

Freakin' brilliant!

CHAPTER 63—*True Lies*, the movie

I'm going to lump the actors all together here and just mention that they all flew into Key West from all points north and west, were picked up in limousines and were shuttled over to the opulence that is the Pier House for the duration of their shoot.

Then, every morning, at the crack of blackness, they were unceremoniously wretched from their slumber hustled out and dumped in a caravan of limos of various vintage and color and whisked north to the day's shooting locations of Sugarloaf, Marathon, the Seven Mile Bridge, and dangling from a whirring helicopter.

And sometimes "people of power and wealth" forget that HOW THEY TREAT the "little people" will not be soon forgotten.

Certainly not down here in Key West.

This noted from various limo drivers:

Jamie Lee Curtis—"A sweetheart, funny, cheerful, and respectful, all this in a killer body."

Arnold Schwarzenegger—"Big! Polite, just damn nice. Really enjoyed the pool at the Pier House.:

James Cameron—the director of *True Lies*, "quiet, intelligent." (Must have enjoyed filming and living near the water as he would go on to direct *Titanic* just a few years later.)

Tom Arnold—"A first-class arrogant schmuck. Talked down to everyone, insulted everyone." (Guess what, Tom Arnold? You're not welcome back in Key West!)

Jamie Lee and Arnie and James Cameron, you can come back whenever you want.

**FY-awards-I: Jamie Lee Curtis won a Golden Globe Award for Best Actress for her work in this film.

CHAPTER 64—David Robinson

You remember David Robinson, "The Admiral," professional basketball player, Olympian, member of the Dream Team, with two Gold Medals and one Bronze, Naval Academy, all-around cool dude.

He was born in Key West on 6 August 1965, and played basketball for only one year while in high school.

With not much of a track record to show, he was not recruited by major basketball schools.

Their loss.

So he enrolled at the Naval Academy and sprouted from a lanky 6-6 to a well-muscled rebound-and-scoring machine 7-1.

David Robinson, the late-bloomer that nobody wanted, ended up being the College Player of the Year, the #1 overall pick in the 1987 NBA Draft, Rookie Player of the Year, MVP, Defensive Player of the Year.

Not too shabby for a skinny kid from the rock.

CHAPTER 65—Sam Hochman

Sam was our landlord when we lived at 704 Caroline, and Shel Silverstein's carousing partner in crime. Sam paid the price of good-living and excess in all forms and ended up with COPD. We were walking with him the 8 minutes to the post office one morning and he just couldn't breathe and he couldn't keep up. We slowed down to a snail's. It took us over 20 minutes. Sam had to give up smoking and drinking and told me: "Life just isn't fun anymore."

I wanted to put Sam in here to honor him. He was so good to us.

R.I.P. dear Sam, if you ended up in Heaven, try to behave, if you ended up in Hell, well, then just be you.

CHAPTER 66—JFK

Kennedy visited Key West *twice*, for a combined total of just under nine hours.

In 1961, on the first visit, he met with British Prime Minister Macmillan in Truman Annex. Harold Evans, the British equivalent of Press Secretary Pierre Salinger, was stunned and gobsmacked, by the informality of Kennedy during the lunch break when JFK said: "the only thing keeping his headaches at bay was regular sex."

On November 26th, 1962, in his Key West speech, Kennedy thanked the Navy, Air Force and Marine fliers whose reconnaissance flights over Cuba during the missile crisis "played the most important and the most critical part in the most dangerous days that America has faced since the end of World War II."

JFK was a BIG cigar aficionado. He loved various brands, but he loved Cuban cigars the most.

Indeed, he loved Cuban cigars so much, he asked Press Secretary, and fellow cigar aficionado, Pierre Salinger to acquire 1000 hand-rolled "Petit Upmanns" just hours before he signed the embargo on Cuba, from that point the cigars would then be illegal contraband.

Here's what Pierre Salinger said about the request: "The next morning, I walked into my White House office at about 8am, and the direct line from the President's office was already ringing. He asked me to come in immediately.

"'How did you do Pierre?' he asked, as I walked through the door. 'Very well,' I answered. In fact, I'd gotten 1,200 cigars. Kennedy smiled, and opened up his desk.

"He took out a long paper which he immediately signed. It was the decree banning all Cuban products from the United States. Cuban cigars were now illegal in our country."

CHAPTER 67—Fidel Castro

Castro paid a visit to Miami on three different occasions.

In 1948, he came on his honeymoon.

In 1949, he came to hide.

In 1955, he came to drum up support from Cuban exiles.

And on two of those occasions he came down to Key West.

When Castro honeymooned in October of 1948, with his young bride Mirta Díaz-Balart, he wanted to stay in "the finest hotel on Miami Beach," but upmarket choices were limited back then to but a few on the beachfront side of Collins Avenue: the opulent Shelborne, the Saxony which was only just completed, and the still under construction Sans Souci.

Castro met his bride at the University of Havana where she was studying Philosophy and Literature, and he was studying Law. She just happened to be the sister of his University of Havana Law School classmate and close friend, Rafael Díaz-Balart, the father of present-day Miami politicians Lincoln and Mario Diaz-Balart.

FLASHBACK: Lincoln Diaz-Balart was active in the attempt by relatives of Elian Gonzalez (who came over on a raft, where his mother lost her life) to gain custody of the six-year-old from his Cuban father.

After ten days honeymooning in Miami Beach, swimming in the ocean, swimming in the big pool, and living the American highlife, Castro and his bride peregrinated north to New York City. In Manhattan, they stayed with Fidel's old university friend Díaz-Balart and his wife, Hilda, in a tiny apartment on the Upper West Side at West 82nd Street.

Castro wanted to improve his English and visit the many bookstores, so they stayed on and rented a room in the same building.

Apparently, you can only take the company of close relatives for so long.

Castro was mesmerized by the vibrancy and affluence of New York and yearned to somehow be part of that, so he went out and purchased a shiny 1947 Lincoln Continental which sported a feature he had never seen in an automobile before— "power windows." Castro paid in cash, using a portion of the *dólares* he had been given as a wedding gift by his father-in-law.

After several weeks in New York, and now running out of money, (sell the Lincoln Continental, Fidel!) the lovebirds loaded the Díaz-Balarts into the flash wheels and headed back to Miami, taking U.S. 1 all the way to South Florida. In Miami, Castro dropped off the Díaz-Balarts at the airport, where they caught a plane back home to Havana.

Then Castro and his bride carried on south down the Overseas Highway to Key West, where they chilled in the Old Town and soon boarded a ferry back to Havana.

And, yes, they took the Lincoln Continental back to Cuba with them.

It's probably still running.

On Castro's second trip to Miami, when he came to hide, he did so as he feared for his life. This was in November of 1949, you see—big surprise—Castro had a nasty reputation as a political thug at the University of Havana. He feuded with his enemies. He denounced them publicly and then he got skittish and feared they would kick his ass, or worse.

That can be the end result when you're a big bully.

Castro returned to Miami again, in 1955, to plot a revolution. "A young Cuban revolutionary is in Miami making plans to topple the government of Fulgencio Batista," reported the intrepid *Miami Herald*.

It quoted Castro as saying: "We have an organized movement of 100,000 persons. If Batista continues to remain in power by force, then there is no other way but to remove him by force."

Castro spoke at rallies in Miami Beach, Little Havana, and at the rundown Flagler Street Theater and was roundly applauded and well-received.

Then Castro was struck with a brainstorm: He felt it prudent to hit up other communities where there was a substantial Cuban enclave (and money), so after Miami, he traveled up to Tampa and then, you guessed it, he came back down here to Key West.

Castro was a student of history and was keen to speak at the historic San Carlos Institute on Duval Street from the same balcony where Cuban patriot Martí had spoken to Cuban cigar makers who worked here and who had fought for liberation from Spain decades earlier.

This would garner him another photograph in the newspaper!

But Castro's request was denied.

True to his mercurial and rebellious nature, Castro scarpered to Stock Island and held his rally there, spewing his rhetoric, requesting financial support, and denigrating the San Carlos' decision to give him the cold shoulder. Oddly, his histrionics fell on deaf ears, and he exited stage south.

You win some, and sometimes you get a kick in the *cojones*.

And we all know the rest of the story.

Or do we?

Fidel Castro did NOT live a life of dire Cuban austerity, rather a decadent one of opulence: He had his very own private island called Cayo Piedra off the south coast of Cuba (near the Bay of Pigs), a private yacht, over twenty homes. And get this: over a decade ago, *Forbes* estimated Fidel Castro's personal net worth at $900 million. That's a lot of communist rationing for one person.

And this at a time when the average Cuban was only pulling down about $20 a month.

CHAPTER 68—Colin Powell

In 2001, retired four-star general and then Secretary of State, Colin Powell jetted down to Key West to lead international peace talks between the presidents of Azerbaijan and Armenia, who had been stressing big time over a chunk of land.

As one does.

These talks were held at the Little White House in Truman Annex.

Why Key West? you ask.

I was asking myself the same question. I wasn't there at the Little White House to give you a definitive answer, but I was probably at The Bull then, thinking about it all, and I will now let you in on what I thought back in 2001.

The previous two meetings between these opposing factions had taken place in Paris in January and in March.

Have you ever been to Paris in January?

In March?

You froze your bahookie off, didn't you? That glorious mid-winter temperature in icy climes when it doesn't know if it should snow or rain, so it throws SLEET at you and adds a brisk damp waft coming off the Seine to slap you across the face and find its way down the back of your neck, even though you spent a suitable amount of time wrapping that new "Paris Saint-Germain" scarf around your throat in fetching continental fashion.

Remember, there's no bad weather…just a bad choice of clothing.

In 2001, on 26-27 January (the offending dates), Paris had a high of 46F and a low of 39, and the wind was a frisky 31mph. That converts to a wind chill of roughly 27F.

This is why the French invented cognac and calvados, embraced the duvet, and excel at *amour*.

143

On 4-5 March, the weather was worse.

So when someone suggested Key West, FL, there must have been a resounding: "I'm in!"

Check out this video of the president of Azerbaijan and his entourage arriving in Key West by private jet.

https://www.youtube.com/watch?v=_NpPwtDMxwg

Observe the folk in serious suits and ties clamoring off the airplane. Then watch the Duval Street action. The Little White House action. Eventually, you'll be taken back to the airport where passengers *in suits* are now piling off the private jet from Armenia. Where are all the women? Keep your eyes peeled for that particularly young lad carrying the fat briefcase.

I'm thinking family member.

I'm thinking he does NOT have some top secret dossiers in that briefcase.

I'm thinking flip flops, suntan lotion, un-opened box of condoms, and a shaker of salt (as there was no check by customs on account of the usual diplomatic immunity doo dah).

What?

What's that you're asking?

What was the weather like in Key West on 3 April when the peace talks were held?

I just happen to have that right here at my fingertips: High 81 and the Low 73.

Oh, and the ocean was an exceedingly agreeable bath-like 78F.

CHAPTER 69—Boog Powell

And, yes, you are correct in the assumption that there is no relation to the aforementioned Colin.

In his day, *this* Powell was one of major league baseball's great sluggers. An absolute Paul Bunyan of a man standing six-feet-four and weighing in at a rippling-in-muscles 240 pounds.

Boog was BIG.

Colorful sports broadcaster Joe Garagiola once quipped: "If Boog Powell held out his arm, he'd be a railroad crossing."

That's big.

Boog Powell moved to Key West (from Lakeland, FL) with his father and two younger brothers when he was 15, attended Key West High School, and was a three-sport star in football, basketball and baseball.

He graduated in 1959, and had numerous college football scholarships, but had his heart set on playing baseball. At the age of 17, based on glowing-scouting reports, the Baltimore Orioles offered Boog a $35,000 bonus to play in their farm system.

Thirty-five-thousand big ones in 1959, not bad for a kid out of Key West High.

Powell said he received his odd nickname, Boog, from his father. "In the South they call little kids who are often getting into mischief boogers, and my dad shortened it to Boog.

As you can imagine, Key West in the late-50s was a sleepy little town and Boog and his two younger brothers grew up in an old conch house that had been built in the 1800s out of durable Dade County pine.

Boog's mother had died when he was just ten, and his father made darn sure his boys took advantage of growing up in some place as rich in outdoor activity as the Florida Keys.

Boog reminisced: "We kids learned to swim, fish and snorkel. One of my favorite things was diving for lobsters.

You'd go down less than 10 feet and bring one up. I still enjoy that, and if I'm not there for the start of the lobster season, I miss it."

Boog Powell powered the Baltimore Orioles to three straight World Series.

Boog Powell was the first Baltimore Orioles hitter to lead the American League in slugging percentage when he edged out Mickey Mantle (.591) with a .606 slugging percentage in 1964.

He was one of the few players to ever win both a Little League World Series and the Major League World Series.

He used to own a marina on Stock Island.

And he still calls Key West home.

"I love it down here. Even if you forget a name, everybody just smiles and waves and says, Hey Bubba!"

**ASSIGNMENT FOR YOU: Hop on your Conch Cruiser and pedal on over to Rex Weech Field where the Conchs play their baseball and have a peep at what's written off behind the batting cage.

CHAPTER 70—Thomas Edison

Let me set the stage (and illuminate it, as well).

Up until 1897, streets in Key West had gas streetlights.

Then change slowly came about with Duval and a few other streets having their gas streetlights converted to electric streetlights.

Thomas Alva Edison wintered in Fort Myers and thought to himself "Why don't I just jump on the ferry at Punta Rassa and go on down to Key West and have a good nose around and see what all the fuss is about."

Those are possibly not his exact words.

The year of 1897 just also happened to be when a certain local judge and attorney Jeptha Vining Harris built the Southernmost House at the Atlantic end of Duval for an eye-watering $250,000.

Now, a young lassie by the name of "Florida" Curry (appropriate Christian name, wouldn't you say?) was Judge Harris' devoted wife and was just hankering to put her stamp on the house (yes, hankering).

Can you see where this is going?

Florida Curry was the youngest daughter of William Curry (think Curry Mansion, on Caroline Street) and, yes, she wanted the luxury and novelty of her home-sweet-home to be the first on the island to have the luxury of lights.

That would certainly up her street cred.

Florida Curry got wind that Thomas Edison was poking around the island and invited him over and probably said something like "Work your magic, Electric Man!"

Possibly not her exact words.

Well, our Thomas not only personally oversaw the electrical design of the grand manse, but the installation of all wiring, fancy fixtures, fiddly plugs and hard-to-reach sockets, as well.

Florida Curry didn't settle for second best.

With her money, she didn't need to.

Can't you just hear the neighbors conversing over the back fence? Or in this case, the back plumeria bush.

"Hey, neighbor, I hear you're getting electricity. Who do you have doing the lighting?"

"I got Bubba Switch, from the bait shop over on Stock Island. He says 'How hard can it be?'"

"Bubba Switch? Can't say that I know him…"

"Y'know, Bubba from Bait & Switch over there by the shrimp docks. Says he's real cheap and he'll turn up sober. Who you got, Judge?"

"I got Thomas Edison."

"Jesus H. Christ."

"Indeed."

* * *

Wait, there's more!

On 21 April 1898, Thomas Edison shot the first movie to be filmed on location in Key West.

In the following clip, you will see five different scenes, spanning two years:

—a procession of caskets bearing the deceased sailors, victims of the sinking of the *Maine*, being drawn by horse and led by horse and carriage down Duval on the way to the Key West cemetery where their remains were to be interred.

—the dispatch ship *Buccaneer* cleaving the Key West harbor upon entry (the dispatch ships were employed to bring news from Havana to war correspondents waiting in Key West).

—the next scene is of a group of war correspondents pushing and shoving one another as they rush down Duval Street to relay updates about the Spanish-American War to their respective news' outlets.

—then, a shot of the battleship *Indiana* entering the Key West harbor.

—and finally, Edison's scenes shot from aboard a steamship out in bad weather and heavy seas, filmed in the Florida Straits between Key West and Havana.

Take a peek here to see this historic series, and be patient with the quality on offer, it's grainy and jerky: https://www.youtube.com/watch?v=dx0m5piR1Gg

* * *

Edison yearned to return to Key West, and he finally did in 1917/18 as the head of the U.S. Navy Consulting Board. He hung out for six months in what is now known as the Little White House. The complex was built in 1890, (and was right on the water back then), as housing for two-families, the base commandant and his trusty paymaster. The building was referred to as "Quarters A and B."

In case you're wondering, the structure was converted into a single-family dwelling in 1911.

While residing in Key West, Thomas Edison was credited with improving, designing and perfecting 41 weapons for the US war effort, including experiments regarding an underwater listening device to detect enemy ships.

The man certainly his head screwed on the right way.

JOKE: (this will make you groan): How many geniuses does it take to screw in a lightbulb?
ANSWER: Just one, Thomas Edison.
Groan.

To unwind, Thomas Edison spent many evenings at the Monroe Theater, where he had the same reserved seat for each show.

What forward thinking.

Despite two marriages, rumors swirled about Edison's sexuality.

Why? you ask.

Probably because the first motion picture he ever made starred two men embracing and dancing as a third man played the violin.

Might have been less suspicious if there had been no strings attached.

Groan.

**X-RATED NOTE: The Monroe Theater was a movie house, and before that a theatre for theatrical plays and "agreeable musical entertainment fayre."

The Monroe was built in 1912.

As a movie theatre, it was big on Tom Mix films, Rock Hudson films, and a fair amount of hardcore porn. In the 1970s, the Monroe was showing generic porn during the day, *The Devil and Mrs. Jones*, and then *Deep Throat* at night. Difficult to swallow, I know, but I tell the honest truth, ask the hundreds upon hundreds of randy sailors who, ah, came here…over and over again.

**AUTHOR'S oops! NOTE: In my never-ending quest to bring you the truth through in-your-face research, I must confess that I had a cheeky sneaky peek at the trailer for *Deep Throat*. On account of it being a trailer, much is intimated, mind you, but nevertheless it doesn't take a lot of imagination to assess and determine what is transpiring.

And guess what?

In one of the steamy scenes (aren't they all), Linda Lovelace was doing it in proper southern-European fashion, on the same brand, same style, and same color of sheets that I possessed in my modest flat in the '70s. Shock-horror. I must admit here and I will only mention it if you can keep a secret, I apparently had pretty bad taste in sheets in the '70s. Y'know, those brown swirly ones that look as if the designer had been on a particularly bad acid trip?

At least my sheets didn't have the stains.

**ELECTRICITY IN KEY WEST NOTE: In those early days of electricity, the "Key West Electric Company" was a completely private firm led by John Jay Philbrick. And because this was pure capitalism, a competing electric company formed, composed of Charles Curry, Martin L. Hellings, Milton W. Curry, George H. Curry and Joseph Y. Porter—all sons or sons-in-law of millionaire William Curry. By late 1897, "William Curry's Sons Company" went online with their own electric plant, at first serving only their own homes and a few customers, but soon it became a serious rival to Philbrick's. This meant that for a period of time, there were *two* competing electric companies in Key West, each with their own sets of poles, wires and unique infrastructure.

In 1900, Key West was running electric streetcars.

CHAPTER 71—Mel Fisher

Treasure hunter.

Key West legend.

"King" of the Conch Republic *four* times. (This is a seriously lofty position, might I add, right up there with the heads of state of other bacchanal micro-nations.)

If you've followed Mel Fisher's journey, you probably know much of it already. For those of you who don't, I present you with the economical version: Mel was born in Hobart, Indiana (that's just south of Gary), in 1922, served in World War II with the U.S. Army Corps of Engineers, and after the war moved about the country trying various lines of work, finally ending up on his parents' chicken farm in Torrance, California, a suburb of L.A.

Raising chickens may not have been on his bucket list, but this may have been a sign that Key West, ah, lay in his future.

Fisher loved the ocean, so while still raising 10,000 chickens, slinging chicken shit and chasing after peeps, he opened up a "dive shop" in the feed store at the chicken ranch, where he installed a compressor, filled tanks, and sold any diving gear he could get his hands on.

Eventually, Mel's parents put the chicken farm on the market and it drew the interest of a "family" from Montana, and they ended up buying the whole chicken-wire shebang. When I say "family," it was a family of sorts, a mother and her good-looking daughters, plus an uncle.

Hmm.

When the family arrived with daughters in tow, Mel took one look at the flaming redhead by the name of Dolores (nicknamed "Deo") and was hit by the thunderbolt.

It was love at first sight.

Two years later, they were married.

The lovebirds honeymooned in Florida and dove on shipwrecks.

Are you getting the back story here?

Can you see into the future?

When they returned to Southern California, they dove commercially for spiny lobsters and sold them to local restaurants (which was quite lucrative). They saved their money religiously and opened up a proper dive shop in December of 1953 on Catalina Avenue in Redondo Beach, not far from the pier. The shop was appropriately called "Mel's Aqua Shop."

It's often claimed that Mel's Aqua Shop was the "world's very first dive shop," but it wasn't even the first dive shop in California.

Or even the first dive shop in L.A.

That honor went to "Dive N' Surf" in neighboring Hermosa Beach.

Mel and Deo started a family and they expanded their business, teaching scuba to thousands of enthusiasts, and shooting underwater footage for educational porpoises, I mean purposes and the big silver screen.

On a dive trip to the Caribbean, Fisher met treasure hunter Kip Wagner who was in the hunt for nearly a dozen Spanish ships from the year 1715 that had gone down off the "Treasure Coast" of Florida.

Fisher and Wagner became partners and agreed to search for one year without pay, but near the end of that one year they had not struck gold, rather they had struck out.

That's when Mel Fisher had a life-changing brainstorm. He was watching the powerful engines on his dive boat churn the aqua-marine water with its props one day, and BANG an idea! He reckoned that if he could securely anchor the dive boat above where they thought a wreck might be, and then deflect the "wash" of the boat's props downward instead of out, it might just clear away all the silt in the water that his divers were stirring up as they scoured the seabed.

Mel constructed a large, elbow-shaped cylinder of sorts, much larger than a garbage can, that would fit over the props and direct the surging force of the water downward much like you do when you use the pressure washer on all that dirty oil on your driveway (which now looks mighty fine, I have to tell you).

To Mel's surprise, not only did the force from the "blow" clear away the silt hanging in the water, it raked and scoured and created large craters in the ocean floor removing both sediment and vegetation in a matter of seconds WHOOSH! and suddenly before them in the crystal-clear Atlantic waters was a glittering, beckoning trove of 1,033 gold doubloons.

This blasting the ocean floor away technique, was colloquially called the "mailbox method," or just "mailboxing," (it delivers?) and is still used to search for treasure on the ocean floor today.

Smart thinking, our Mel, here was a man who had a dream, had resolute optimism, and thought clearly on his very tanned feet.

But this treasure find had taken place off the east coast of Florida and the east coast had a narrow window for diving and treasure hunting as the water was too rough in the winter months, so Mel and Deo and family upped anchor and moved to the Keys, with their eyes set on finding the ultimate prize: the *Nuestra Señora de Atocha*, a Spanish galleon that had sunk in a hurricane in 1622 along with its sister-ship the *Santa Margarita*.

The *Atocha* had gone down with 260 passengers and crew.

**AUTHOR'S shipwrecked NOTE: There were five survivors from the *Atocha*: 3 crew and two slaves who had clung to the broken mizzen mast.

The ship had been carrying riches from the Spanish colonial ports of Cartagena, and Porto Bello in New Granada (present-day Columbia), and Panama, Peru, Mexico and Havana, and was headed for Spain: 125 gold bars and discs, 24 tons of silver bullion in the form of 1038 ingots, 180,000 silver coins, 582 copper ingots, 350 chests of indigo, 525 bales of tobacco, 1200 pounds of engraved silverware and 71 pounds of rare "Muzo" emeralds and other precious stones.

Along with what was officially recorded in the manifest, there were unknown amounts of contraband gold "boot bars" and even uncut emeralds secreted out of Columbia.

The Spaniards undertook salvage operations for several years (remember, this is back in the 1600s) by employing Indian slaves as divers, and recovered nearly half of the cargo from the holds of the *Atocha's* sister-ship the *Santa Margarita*.

Many Indian slaves perished during the recovery of a portion of the *Santa Margarita's* booty as they went down inside a brass bell with a single window, and they had no experience in diving. Many couldn't even swim.

Dead slaves were recorded as a business expense by the captains of salvage ships.

The *Atocha* had been lost in deeper waters and strewn a distance by a second hurricane. It was never found, but the Spanish thought they knew roughly where both ships had come to rest and their positions had been documented.

Spanish records placed the wreck of the *Santa Margarita* and the *Atocha* off "Matecumbe," so Mel Fisher and his divers searched for years off Upper and Lower Matecumbe Key, near Islamorada, only to learn that the Spanish called ALL the Keys "Matecumbe."

Remember this is the short version.

To strengthen his team and ensure his operation was more appealing to his now 700 investors, Fisher enlisted the aid of a marine archeologist and a PhD candidate who traveled to Seville in Spain. In Seville, worm-eaten documents were unearthed and they bore these Spanish words "*Cayos del Marques*."

The Marquesas!

Mel Fisher rebooted and moved his entire operation and now armada of rickety vessels down to Key West and began searching off the Marquesas, 100 miles farther on toward the setting sun.

For a combined total of sixteen years, do I need to say that again SIXTEEN YEARS, Mel, Deo, and their brood of five children, Dirk, Terry, Kim, Kane, and Taffi searched relentlessly for the *Atocha* with only a few minor finds.

Then, in 1973, Mel and his crew unearthed three silver bars matching the weight and tally numbers from the *Atocha's* manifest.

Then, in 1975, Mel's son Dirk discovered nine bronze

cannons that he believed were also from the *Atocha*.

Also in 1975, a large amount of the mother lode from the *Santa Margarita*, where some $20 million in gold was waiting, was discovered by Mel's other son, Kane.

Then…on the night of 19 July, 1975, the rust-bucket of a boat that was skippered by Mel's oldest son Dirk, a 60-foot converted Mississippi tugboat, christened the *Northwind,* had a failure in a toilet fitting, water surged into the bilge, the boat listed. Fuel from the starboard tank poured into the port tank.

The boat listed more.

Dirk and his wife Angel were asleep in an air-conditioned cabin, four divers were asleep in the crew quarters forward, five more divers were asleep up on the deck in the open air. The boat listed yet more, no one woke, then it rolled and capsized.

Donnie Jones, a diver from Key West, ended up trapped in the engine room for 8 minutes in an air pocket. He somehow located a flashlight and was able to escape the sinking vessel by swimming through the blackness and out.

Dirk and Angel and diver Rick Gage never made it out.

The accident happened about 5.30am. When divers on a neighboring boat anchored a distance away awoke around 8.00am, they noticed that the *Northwind* was no longer there. And then they saw the survivors in the water clinging to debris.

Deo wanted to throw in the towel.

Mel said Dirk would have wanted them to continue. He told his wife: "It's a powerful ocean. It takes people and ships."

So they carried on.

On 20 July 1985, ten agonizing years to the day later, Kane and the crew found a massive collection of silver bars that matched the manifest of *Nuestra Señora de Atocha*.

And the *Atocha* began to begrudgingly give up her cargo with a value of over $450 million ("1985" dollars).

And Mel Fisher's dream came true.

Now for something that I recently learned, and I will leave it up to you to decide how you feel about the effect it has on Mel Fisher's legacy:

Near the end of Mel Fisher's fairytale life he was accused of fraud and "salting" the wreck site. Without investors it would have been nigh impossible to carry on the protracted search for treasure. The expense was simply prohibitive. But without the occasional success, there would be no investors. Investors wanted results. And they only wanted to invest in diving companies that were bringing returns.

This, from *The New York Times* back in 1998:

"Treasure hunter Mel Fisher has admitted selling several counterfeit gold coins at his gift shop here (in Key West) and has agreed to repay customers their purchase prices of $2,500 to $10,000.

"In a negotiated plea, Fisher's company also agreed that in the future it would sell only coins recovered from shipwrecks for which it has federal salvage rights. The coins in question were said to have been purchased from a longtime colleague who had contended that they were genuine. The agreement, signed Nov. 18, tarnished a career in which Fisher found hundreds of thousands of gold and silver coins, bars and jewelry from Spanish shipwrecks off Florida. He and several investors became millionaires from a haul valued at more than $400 million.

"Fisher, whose office was raided by police in April, is near death from cancer, said a lawyer, Michael Halpern, who negotiated the plea for Crystals of Delaware, Fisher's retail sales subsidiary. Halpern said he believed Fisher's illness contributed to the fraud. 'He was taking immense amounts of medicine,' Halpern said. 'He is very, very vulnerable.'

"Fisher's son, Kim, who is running the company, signed the plea bargain for his father.

"Under the agreement, Crystals pleaded no contest but acknowledged that the coins were not from a 1733 Spanish fleet that went aground near the Florida Keys.

"In addition to the more than $67,000 to be paid to identified claimants, the company agreed to maintain a $50,000 restitution fund for any additional customers who demand refunds during the three-year probation period.

"Paul Myers, an investigator for the Monroe County state's attorney's office, said he found indications that as many as 1,000 counterfeit coins bearing a 1733 fleet insignia were forged over the past 25 years and may have been sold by other dealers.

"'Fisher bought the coins from Walter Kruse, a longtime treasure-hunting associate with a criminal record of selling fake coins,' Myers said. 'Fisher sold the coins with a signed certificate stating that he had found them.'

"Halpern said the agreement to sell only coins from Fisher's six Florida shipwreck sites protects both customers and Fisher's reputation. Under federal salvage law, found treasure is presented to a federal judge who certifies authenticity and title and insures that archaeological rules were followed."

What's more, Mel Fisher's company was fined $500,000 for destroying more than an acre of protected sea grass off the Florida Keys while looking for shipwrecks.

Mr. Fisher was treated for lymphoma with months of chemotherapy, and died at his home in Key West on 19 December 1998.

Mel Fisher requested that his ashes be scattered along "Kane's Trail," a 7.5-mile stretch of ocean floor from the site where the first silver coin from the *Atocha* was found in 1971 to the site of the mother lode in 1985.

CHAPTER 72—John James Audubon

Audubon was born on April 26, 1785, on a sugarcane plantation in Les Cayes, Saint-Domingue, Hispaniola. This was a former French colony, from 1659 to 1804, and is what we now know as Haiti.

Audubon's father, Captain Jean Audubon, was a French plantation owner and slave master. His mother was one of the captain's mistresses, a Creole chambermaid by the name of Jeanne Rabin(e).

Audubon was christened "Jean Rabin" at birth. When his mother died shortly thereafter, he was shipped off to Nantes, France, where he was raised by the captain's long-suffering wife, Anne.

Audubon was legally registered by his father and stepmother in 1794, and overnight he went from "Jean Rabin illegitimate child" to Jean-Jacques Fougère Audubon, child of privilege.

In 1803, when Audubon was 18, war broke out between France and England. To keep young Jean from being conscripted into the Emperor Napoleon's army, his father acquired a false passport for his dear son and sent him to his estate in Mill Grove, Pennsylvania.

Before arriving on our shoes, Audubon anglicized his name to John James Audubon.

Round about 1819, Audubon was having serious financial difficulties, went bankrupt and was thrown into the slammer for outstanding debt. The little money he did earn at the time was from the grisly task of drawing "death-bed sketches," greatly sought after by country folk prior to the, ah, development of photography.

By May of 1832, John James Audubon had turned his life around, reinvented himself, and had become America's foremost naturalist and bird artist. He often shot and killed the colorful birds in order to keep them still enough to sketch and paint.

Audubon got wind of the plethora of bird species which called the Florida Keys home, so he set sail for Key West.

He and his party arrived in Key West on May 4th, on the US Revenue Cutter *Marion*.

In Key West, Audubon had a letter of introduction to Dr. Benjamin Strobel, who had a modest house on the seven-acre property on which the present-day Audubon House sits. At the time, the entire property was owned by Pardon Greene (think "Greene Street"), one of Key West's founding fathers. Captain John Huling Geiger (wrecker and maritime pilot), rented a house on the property, as well. Geiger eventually bought the property after a hurricane destroyed most of the homes on the island.

Between 1846 and 1849, Geiger built the house we now call the Audubon House. Geiger employed ships' carpenters and built with durable Dade County pine, cypress and mahogany. The home had unobstructed views of the sea back then (before the Custom House was built and blocked it), and it granted Geiger the perfect vantage point to keep an eye on the reef and a lookout for shipwrecks.

* * *

Audubon sailed to the Dry Tortugas on May 10. He remained in the islands until May 16.

On an island called Bird Key, Audubon and his colleagues encountered a crew of "eggers" from Havana, who were there to gather the eggs of Sooty Terns, Black Skimmers and Brown Noddys from their nests on the Tortugas and sail with them back to Havana, where they would be sold for a good price.

Audubon hung out in Key West until May 22, then aimed north stopping briefly at Indian Key (mile marker 78.5) before sailing on to Charleston.

FOWL NOTE: Today the Dry Tortugas are on the main flyway for birds migrating from Cuba and Central America northward to the United States and beyond.

In October 1846, a powerful hurricane bore down on Key West, damaging or destroying nearly all of the homes in the city.

In the aftermath of this devastating storm, our Capt. Geiger, a harbor pilot and master wrecker, began construction on a grand home that would serve as his family's residence. Today, that home is known as the Audubon House.

Okay, listen up everybody, time to spill out of all the Duval Street bars. Who wants to jump on their bikes? I've got something I want to show you.

Meet me at the corner of Greene and Whitehead Street, by the house with the white picket fence.

Go!

How did you beat me here? It must've been because I stopped by the Key Lime Pie Bakery on Greene Street for a Key lime ice cream.

Okay, as you've all figured out all on your own by now, we are standing in front of the Audubon House. Beautiful, isn't it? It's an exquisite example of American Classic Revival architecture.

Okay, now set your peepers on the large metal engraved historical marker just here in front of us. The one stuck in the ground by the Historical Association of Southern Florida.

See where it says the house was built in 1830? Hmm.

Is that a typo, I wonder?

This house wasn't built until the 1840s. That's even clarified on the Audubon House's own website. Or on the tour.

Hmm, again.

And then it says, as you can see, that John James Audubon was hosted here in 1832. Hmm, again, not possible if the house wasn't built until nearly a decade later. Perhaps he was "hosted" in one of the dwellings that was on the property back then?

But I'm not here to disparage someone's nonprofit educational organization, so I will just say that the Audubon House has many fine prints and originals from the famous ornithologist on display inside, and the interior of the house itself is a glorious example of the construction that was done by ships' carpenters back in the 1840s.

And the garden is to die for. All the plants are labeled, so you learn quite a fair amount and improve your brain at the same time.

CHAPTER 73—Goldie Hawn

If you haven't seen the 1992 movie *CrissCross* she filmed here on the island and at Eden House, stop reading right now and download it. It captures a moderately gentle, somewhat innocent, sometimes not so innocent, time gone by.

Filming took place over the summer of 1990.

And you can *feel* the heat.

Scott Summers wrote the short story *CrissCross* while staying at Eden House in early 1976.

Pop on over to Eden House if you get the chance. It's just there at 1015 Fleming Street.

Park your bike in the bike rack out front.

They have a lot of cool memorabilia from the movie throughout the art deco hotel.

Definitely worth a snoop.

CHAPTER 74—Stepin Fetchit

Born in Key West on 30 May 1902, just hours after his parents arrived on a boat from the West Indies, one Lincoln Theodore Monroe Andrew Perry was named after four presidents.

His father was a cigar maker, cook, aspiring minstrel, and stage performer from Jamaica.

His mother, a seamstress from Nassau in the Bahamas.

At the age of twelve, young Perry ran away to join a carnival, and for the next eight years tap-danced and sang his way from New York to Los Angeles. The young man was intelligent and he had ambition. By the age of 20, Perry was the manager of his own traveling carnival show.

When he wasn't traveling with his own carnival, Lincoln Perry developed a duo Vaudeville act and took it on the road. The duo were called "Step" and "Fetchit," and the partners worked the "black Vaudeville tour," which was known as the Chitlin Circuit.

When the team broke up, Perry created a solo act and took the stage name "Stepin Fetchit" for himself.

As Stepin Fetchit, he parlayed his rather *fetching* persona into a successful film career, becoming the first black actor to receive featured screen credit in a motion picture, the first black actor to become a box office sensation in the history of cinema, and the first black actor to become a millionaire.

Fetchit had unique longevity in the film business with an exceedingly successful career spanning from 1925 to 1976— more than 50 years.

For his work in the movies, Stepin Fetchit is honored with a Star on the Hollywood Walk of Fame. It can be found at 1751 Vine Street.

From the marl dust of Key West, gold emerges.

CHAPTER 75—Kelly McGillis

Witness with Harrison Ford.

The Accused with Jodie Foster.

Top Gun with Tom Cruise.

Big film star, but then she opted to quit L.A. and move to Key West in the early 1990s, where she loved the heat, loved the humidity, and opened a restaurant (with her then husband Fred Tillman) called…Let's all say it together now: Kelly's.

Kelly's Caribbean Bar, Grill & Brewery was on the corner of Caroline and Whitehead and it was a coveted open-air venue for both visitors and locals.

Kelly McGillis was attracted to the Key West architecture, the historic Old Town, the writers, the artists, the quaint end-of-the-world ambiance, and she could ride her bike around the leafy tropical lanes without being pestered.

The drivers of the Conch Tour Train and the Old Town Trolley were advised: "If you see Kelly McGillis walking down the street, let her be, don't point her out."

"It's got a very European attitude," McGillis said of Key West. "There's a certain tolerance here that's quickly vanishing from the rest of America."

McGillis also owned Kelly's Hanger, a Duval Street clothing boutique. She supported local theatre, she directed productions for the Waterfront Theater and for the Key West Theater Festival. She supported women's flag football (The Kelly McGillis Classic International Women's & Girls' Flag Football).

Kelly eventually sold her restaurant and it became First Flight in 2017.

She divorced Fred Tillman in 2002.

She married Melanie Leis in 2010. They divorced in 2011.

Kelly McGillis now resides in Hendersonville, NC. She is still active in the theatre and the odd independent movie.

CHAPTER 76—Diane Nyad

At the age of 64, on her *fifth* attempt, Diana Nyad became the first person to swim from Cuba to Key West, FL, without a shark cage.

Think about that for a moment the next time you go out to Smathers or down to Ft. Zack to have a splash. Look off to the south, in the direction of Cuba.

It's way, way out there.

Gabrielle and I aren't even ready to do it by boat yet.

When Diana was a young girl growing up in Ft. Lauderdale, the Cuban Revolution took place.

She said this: "When I was a nine-year-old living in Ft. Lauderdale, literally overnight, thousands of exiles flooded into my town. We were suddenly eating Cuban food, dancing salsa in my new friends' living rooms. The mystique ran deep. Already a little swimmer, I was standing on the beach at that time and I asked my mother, who had danced salsa many times with my father at the fabled Hotel Nacional in Havana: 'Mom. Where is it? I know it's out there, but I can't see it.'"

And my mother took my arm and pointed it across the sea.

"There," she said. "Out there. It's right over that horizon. It's so close, you could almost swim there."

And in reference to the **"90 Miles to Cuba"** distance, Nyad says it this way: "To be perfectly accurate, it is 103 miles, the closest distance between Cuba and Florida. A long time ago, the nautical measurement of 90 was assigned, a measurement used exclusively by large ships at sea. We measure distances across the sea between countries in statute miles.

"Trust me, it's 103 miles to Cuba. I should know."

CHAPTER 77—Bill Clinton

"He came to Key West, but he didn't inhale…"

This told to me by a certain musician friend who shall remain nameless so as not to incriminate and sully his reputation, which would of course have a knock-on effect when gigging at Two Friends, Rick's, the Pier House Beach Bar, Smokin' Tuna, and Dante's.

I actually asked if he was sure that Clinton didn't inhale and his response was: "Close, but no cigar."

OMG.

CHAPTER 78—Oprah

Oprah Winfrey threw a birthday party on Sunset Key (500 yards, *más o menos*, off the island of Key West).

For herself.

When I say she "threw a party," I mean to say she more or less rented all the island's cottages for the grand shindig.

It's vital that party-goers have their own private space so they can discretely change out of those sandy bikini bottoms and get into a fresh pair of dry knickers.

Of course the privacy is appealing for a host of other reasons, such as the basis of those rampant rumors about drug abuse and orgies out there on the island, but I've been unable to verify the rumors, so I'm not going to make any mention of the drug abuse and the orgies…

**AUTHOR'S DREDGING UP FACTS NOTE: Round about the turn of the 19th century, the Navy dredged the Key West harbor repeatedly. So what do you do with all that sediment you dredge up?

You create an island. Two actually, Tank Island and Wisteria Island (Christmas Tree Island). The Navy then had designs on using Tank Island to serve as a fuel tank depot during the Cold War. More dredging took place to build passageways for submarines and other large vessels. Subsequently, the Navy "came about 180 degrees" and the plans to erect fuel tanks on, well, Tank Island were scrapped and only two of the twelve planned fuel tanks were completed.

But…fuel lines had already been run from Key West.

And that piqued the interest of developers.

In 1986, the government sold Tank Island and other anchorages in Key West in an auction to developer Pritam Singh.

In 1988, the existing tanks were dismantled but the

remaining fuel lines served as conduits for water, sewage, and utilities. Power cables were later laid alongside the existing fuel pipes.

And in 1994, the island was "purchased from Singh's creditors" and renamed Sunset Key.

How quaint.

And a few years later, Oprah was able to hold her boozy bash, I mean birthday bash, on the island.

CHAPTER 79—Michael Keaton

Keaton stayed at The Gardens on Angela while here in Cayo Hueso.

This from a local limo company: "Shorter than you'd expect. Friendly and flirtatious with our female driver. We had to hold up a sign when we picked him up at the airport that said MICHAEL DOUGLAS.

Michael Douglas does the same to Keaton, it's a running joke between the two.

And this from a local gent whose grandmother worked as a waitress at Pepe's: "Pepe's gets a lot of famous people in there because it's pretty well known. Anyway, Michael Keaton and his "crew" come in one day at around 11:30 a.m. and begin to order breakfast. My grandmother attempts to inform Mr. Keaton that the restaurant is no longer serving breakfast for the day and that he would have to order something off the lunch menu. Mr. Keaton—whose newest movie, *Batman* had just hit big at the box office—didn't seem to care for this policy and told my grandmother that he would, in fact, be ordering breakfast anyway. Again, my grandmother informed Mr. Keaton that his request would not be met. Mr. Keaton looked my grandmother dead in the eye and said, 'Do you know who I am? I'm Batman!'"

Michael Keaton didn't get what he wanted.

But he got what was coming to him.

The manager of Pepe's threw him and his gang the hell out.

CHAPTER 80—Madonna

This from a limo driver at the aforementioned local limo company:

"Took her to Truman Annex several times. Silent as a silent fuck and about as appealing. Never uttered a word. Cold as in cold fish."

CHAPTER 81—Daisy Fuentes

Daisy was born on 17 November 1966, in Havana. When she was just three, her parents fled to Madrid, Spain, to escape Castro's Cuba.

She learned English by watching episodes of *I Love Lucy*. Ricky Ricardo was Cuban, after all.

**AUTHOR'S FOREIGN LANGUAGE TIP: Learning a foreign language from watching popular TV programs is a good, fun way to improve your language. Gabrielle and I learned Spanish by watching old reruns of *Knight Rider* dubbed in Spanish. Now we know how to say in Spanish: "Put your hands in the air!" and "One more move and it's curtains!" and "You're going down for a long time!" As of this writing, we have not had an opportunity to employ any of the above phrases in Spanish.

Daisy Fuentes was a Grand Marshall of Fantasy Fest. Having this honor, she moved into that coveted echelon of other Grand Marshalls such as Capt. Tony, Jimmy Buffett, Kelly McGillis, Cindy Williams, and Diana Nyad.

And lastly, from our friendly local limo driver: "Daisy Fuentes was a tall glass of water! Nice. Great sense of humor. Her suite at the hotel wasn't quite ready, so she held us and drank a cocktail in the limo."

There's hope for mankind.

CHAPTER 82—Robert Redford

Robert Redford was born 18 August 1936, in Santa Monica, CA, and is of English, Scottish, Irish and Scots-Irish ancestry.

Thus the great head of hair.

Redford was down here on the rock filming for the movie *HAVANA* in 89/90. You may recall that scene with him standing along South Roosevelt Boulevard by Smathers Beach looking out across the Florida Straits toward Cuba.

Pedal on out there. You won't see Cuba either, but you'll get a little color on the back of your legs, which you could use.

Just saying.

CHAPTER 83—Henry Flagler

Henry Morrison Flagler was born on 2 January 1830. He co-founded Standard Oil with partners John D. Rockefeller and Samuel Andrews. By the time he'd reached retirement age, he wasn't ready for the couch, he was simply ready for a change.

Plus, like "Sheldon," he liked trains.

And it goes like this, also harvested from *Key West, Part II, the Seagull, I mean the Sequel*: "Flagler was living in the Great White North and his wife's doctor suggested they winter in Florida due to her failing health. Flagler chose Jacksonville as it was difficult to travel much farther south because the St. Johns River was in the way. Two years later, Flagler's wife died and, with some difficulty, he made his way down to St. Augustine.

"He was taken with St. Augustine's charm, but felt the city was lacking a great hotel, so he built the 540-room Ponce de León Hotel. After he built the Ponce de León, he realized it was still difficult to get to his hotel, so he purchased short line railroads in what would later become known as the Florida East Coast Railway.

The Ponce de León Hotel, now part of Flagler College, opened its doors on 10 January 1888, and was such a success it gave Flagler ideas, big ideas, and he now wanted to create the American Riviera, so he built a railroad bridge across the St. Johns River (do you see where this is going?), so he could gain access to all points south. Then he bought the Hotel Ormond just north of Daytona. And then he constructed the 1,100-room Royal Poinciana Hotel in Palm Beach (the largest wooden structure in the world, at the time). To ensure high occupancy, he went back to the drawing board and extended his railroad all the way to Palm Beach.

Flagler originally intended West Palm Beach to be the terminus of his railroad system, but in 1894 and 1895, severe freezes hit the area, causing Flagler to freeze his ass off and rethink his original decision. Sixty miles south, the town today known as Miami, was untouched by the freeze.

Then the *coup de foudre* was spawned in 1905: Flagler decided that his Florida East Coast Railway should be extended from Biscayne Bay all the way down to Key West.

And at 10.43 a.m., on the 22nd of January 1912, Henry Flagler arrived in his luxurious private coach aboard the first train that chugged down the Overseas Railway, "the railroad that went to sea," and into Key West. In his 80s, in poor health and nearly blind, he de-trained at Trumbo Road and Caroline Street and was greeted by a raucous crowd of more than ten-thousand, made up of foreign dignitaries from Cuba, Navy personnel, local citizens and schoolchildren—all dressed in their Sunday finest, all cheering and waving American flags, reveling in Henry Flagler's fantastic accomplishment.

His impossible dream.

Flagler stood there, motionless, as tears streamed down his face.

"I can hear the children," Flagler said, "but I cannot see them."

Celebrations went on for two weeks, fireworks, parades.

Flagler would die a year later.

Now the entire east coast of Florida, from Jacksonville to Key West, was linked by a single railroad system. Not too bad an effort for a man who really didn't feel that retirement and pottering out in the back garden was for him.

Check out this old black & white photo of Henry Flagler and a few associates on Stock Island:

www.keyshistory.org/SI-Flagler&Party020806.jpg

**BTW: At the end of the line, Flagler needed another grand hotel, so he built the Casa Marina. The Casa Marina confirmed Flagler's belief that Florida and Key West could be transformed from an endless malarial swamp to a paradise.

**YOUR ASSIGNMENT: Slip into The Bull on the corner of Duval and Caroline. Grab a seat at the bar. Who's that portrait, large and life-like, right over there on the wall?

No, not there.

Behind you.

CHAPTER 84—Charles Lindbergh

We all know the side of Lindbergh that was the aviator, the American hero, the military officer, the inventor, and the consultant to Pan American Airways.

And we know about his record-setting flight at the age of only 25, in 1927, when he was the first to fly nonstop from Long Island to Paris—solo—in 33 and ½ hours in the single-engine *Spirit of St. Louis*.

But there was a darker side, as well.

Remember I told you about the nightclub called "Café Cayo Hueso" at the Southernmost House? It was here Charles Lindbergh came, always in the hunt for his next extra-marital affair. To say Lindbergh was quite the ladies' man is hardly strong enough, he was a serial adulterer and even had a complete second family ensconced in Europe. What's more, he had fathered seven children with three German women: three sons with Munich hatmaker Brigitte Hesshaimer, two sons with her sister Marietta, and a son and daughter with his former private secretary Valeska.

Does this sully his reputation?

You decide.

CHAPTER 85—Juan Terry Trippe

Back in early October of 1927, Juan Trippe was up against a deadline to be the "first to deliver Air Mail from Key West to Cuba."

And it HAD to be done by the 19th of October, or he would lose the mail contract.

But Trippe wasn't too worried.

#1 He was the only American who possessed **landing rights** for Campo Columbia airfield in Havana.

#2 He had the coveted U.S. Post Office Air Mail **contract** in hand.

#3 And he had **two** Fokker F-VII tri-motor planes that were due to be delivered to him before the 19th.

They were to be his "airline."

Then the rains came.

Heavy rains, in fact, and those rains inundated Key West and turned the island's Meacham Field (present-day Key West International Airport) into a mosquito-infested backwater swamp. The flooding tore into the marl and limestone upon which Key West is built, and sinkholes puckered the airfield. The sinkholes weren't large, but they were deep. Real deep. One took two tons of rock (that's 400 truckloads worth, to you and me) to fill, and it was only 3-feet wide. As soon as all the holes were filled, the crushed-marl runway was packed hard and smoothed over.

Then the torrential rains came again, flooding the airfield all over again. Remember, Key West is at 26 degrees latitude, in the middle of the sub-tropics—and hurricane season lasts until November 30th.

And now, to make it all somehow worse for Juan Terry Trippe, Campo Columbia airfield in Havana began to flood.

Tick. Tick. Tick. Tick.

It was the 17th of October.

One of Trippe's Fokker aircraft was finally ready to roll, but it could only get as far as Miami. Key West's airfield was still swimming under brackish water and it was a no-go zone for landing.

But Juan T. Trippe was not about to lose everything he'd worked for. Everything he'd dreamed of. And certainly not the Air Mail contract and the $25,000 cash bond deposit as "guarantee of performance."

What to do?

He thought and thought, long and hard, and then he had it, an idea that would save his ass, his upstart airline, and just possibly the future of aviation.

A floatplane…a *seaplane*.

A floatplane could take off from the placid channel bordering the "flats" at Key West and land in the harbor at Havana. Trippe had flown these floatplanes up on Long Island during the summers when he was a young college student at Yale.

Genius.

But where was he going to find a seaplane at the eleventh hour?

On the 18th of October, one day before the dreaded deadline, Trippe learned through the coconut grapevine that a single-engine Fairchild FC-2, which was configured as a *floatplane*, had just diverted to Miami due to an oil leak. The leak was duly fixed and the seaplane was ready to depart, destination Port-au-Prince, Haiti.

In the opposite direction from Key West.

Trippe struck like a viper and offered to charter the seaplane, but the pilot, Cy Caldwell, a feisty Canadian of Scottish descent, balked. He was under contract to West Indian Aerial Express based in the Dominican Republic and had to get back to the island.

Trippe offered money.

Lots of it.

Money speaks.

Cy Caldwell listened, and he had the seaplane in Key West

that very evening, bobbing in the aquamarine waters of the Gulf of Mexico, not far from the foot of Duval.

On the morning of 19 October 1927, a distant rumbling was heard on the island of Key West. It was the mail train chugging down Henry Flagler's Overseas Railway, and onto the rock.

Within minutes the mail was unloaded from the train at Trumbo Point and expeditiously loaded into the single-engine aircraft.

Cy Caldwell fired up the engine, aimed the floatplane south and applied full throttle. The seaplane skimmed the glassy waters off Mallory Dock and Caldwell lifted his 65-horsepower seaplane *La Niña* into the sun-drenched skies above Key West with seven heavy sacks of Air Mail, containing 30,000 letters! He flew across the Florida Straits and the Gulf Stream at an altitude of one-thousand feet and eighty-two minutes later made a smooth landing in Havana's harbor, 103 miles away. There to meet, greet, and complete the delivery was the local Cuban postmaster, who had rowed out to pick up the mail, *on schedule*.

Nothing but net.

Legends made.

An airline born.

Pan American World Airways.

And Key West would not have become the "Birthplace of Pan American World Airways," if not for the quick thinking of one indomitable Juan Terry Trippe.

Trippe would go on and lead Pan Am from 1927 until 1968, and he would expand Pan Am (from the 103 miles to Havana) into a global network of 81,410 miles, to 86 countries and every continent except for Antarctica. Pan Am could take you almost anywhere in the world you wanted to go, and if trouble erupted in the form of an earthquake or hurricane or armed conflict, Pan Am was there to transport in supplies and evacuate the injured and wounded out.

And it all began in Key West, FL.

So, the next time you're down on the island, stroll on over to First Flight Island Restaurant & Brewery (formerly Kelly's) at the corner of Caroline and Whitehead and feast your eyes on the iconic red-and-white sign that proudly states the "Birthplace of PAN AMERICAN WORLD AIRWAYS."

**AUTHOR'S in-flight NOTE: I was lucky enough to work for Pan Am and had the opportunity to fly around the world from east to west and from north to south. To Rio to Beirut to Hong Kong to Teheran to Tokyo to New Delhi to Costa Rica to Honolulu to Kano, Nigeria. I was trained in Miami and based in London, New York, and L.A.

If you want to learn more about Pan Am and the role Key West played, have a peek at my book: *PAN AM—No Sex Please, We're Flight Attendants.*
And PING! don't forget to fasten your seatbelts.

CHAPTER 86—Capt. Tony

Key West is known for its colorful characters.

It attracts them like a magnet.

And it breeds its own.

Capt. Tony could have been the poster child for colorful, larger-than-life characters.

He was a gunrunner, a shrimper, a charter boat captain, the father of thirteen children by eight different women, the owner of his eponymous bar, and a former mayor of Key West.

Tony Tarracino, with the sandpaper voice and the Paul Newman eyes, was born 10 August 1916 in the ghettos of Elizabeth, N.J., where his immigrant father was a bootlegger during Prohibition.

As a youth, Tony felt he needed some sort of part-time job, so he dropped out of school in the ninth grade to make and sell illegal whiskey.

Eventually, he ended up on the wrong side of the New Jersey Mafia, had his head kicked in and was left for dead at the Newark City Dump.

It was 1948, he needed to get out of dodge and had his eyes set on the end of the world—Key West.

Smart move.

First came the charter boat captaincy (which he toiled at for 35 years here).

In 1958, Tony bought the original Sloppy Joe's premises at 428 Greene Street from David Wolkowsky and opened Capt. Tony's Saloon.

You may remember that the bar once doubled as the city morgue (one of the few places on the island that had ice), which was accommodating as locals were dying to get in.

During the 1960s, Capt. Tony became a gunrunner for the U.S. government in support of Cuban mercenaries during the

Bay of Pigs invasion.

In 1985, Capt. Tony ran for mayor of Key West but lost by 52 votes to a banker named Tom Sawyer. Locals joked that the race was "between someone named for a fictional character and someone who *was* a fictional character."

Four years later, Capt. Tony ran again. A lot of folk objected to his frequent use of the word "fuck". Capt. Tony responded to the criticism in his own effable way: "I just hope everybody in Key West who uses that word votes for me. If they do, I'll win in a landslide."

He won.

As mayor of Key West, he sought to "curtail Key West's growth and to keep its reputation as a refuge for eccentrics and renegades who had found their way to the southernmost point of the continental United States."

As mayor, he preserved Key West's daily Sunset Celebration, which made all of us on the pier VERY happy.

He kicked the bucket at the age of 92.

Not a bad run…considering his journey.

A journey which included a diet of pizza and chocolate bars, chain-smoking unfiltered Lucky Strikes, and drinking 12 cups of coffee a day.

MOVIE NOTE: Capt. Tony was portrayed by gutsy and grisly Stuart Whitman in *Cuba Crossing*, a 1980 movie about a band of daring adventurers who get swept up in a plot to kill, you guessed it, Fidel Castro.

CHAPTER 87—Mayor Gonzo Mays

Mayor Gonzo Mays (aka Sammie Mays) is the Official Honorary Mayor of Key West and the Florida Keys.

She's also a journalist (a Gonzo journalist).

A radio show co-host.

A bestselling author.

And a gorgeous cheeky vixen.

So what does it take to become an "Official Honorary Mayor"?

Well, first off, you have to be appointed before you can be anointed.

And it's the County Commission that does that.

And it's a big deal.

A VERY BIG DEAL.

Sammie Mays was bestowed with this honor back in 2008, and she's been rockin' the politically correct boat ever since then, helping to maintain Key West's status as the quirky, funky, eclectic, accepting, end-of-the-world idyll that it has become.

But what else does it take to be the Official Honorary Mayor of Key West? It's important to have been spawned of good stock: "I was strong-headed. My nickname as a child was 'mule'," says Mays, "I came from a background of saloon owners, politicians and the Dixie mafia from New Orleans."

Now if this isn't the right kind of pedigree, then I don't know what is. We all know that Key West is a "sunny place for shady people," so it helps if you have a colorful past.

Even better if that past is delightfully checkered.

As Mayor Gonzo Mays humbly says, puffing on her trademark cigar: "I'm not trying to be Hunter S. Thompson or even Capt. Tony…I'm just interested in giving out as many political favors as humanly possible and accepting all bribes no matter how insignificant."

All mayors should be that honest!

**AUTHOR'S NOTE: Have a squizzy at Sammie's books: *Damn The Carnations: Full Speed Ahead* and *Pirate Night before Christmas*.

And…now you can hear Mayor Gonzo on Radio A1A as she co-hosts with Harry Teaford/Billy Ray Flynn the "The Weekly Trop 40 Countdown."

CHAPTER 88—Freddy Cabanas

Gabrielle and I would be down at Mallory selling our Sunset Photos. We'd be watching Will Soto on the high wire, when our attention would be breached by a speck shooting across the sky, piercing the airspace from the left and the direction of the Key West International Airport.

This, of course, was Freddy rocking along in his Pitts S2-C, soaring high, doing loopy-loops, up there to entertain all of us down below at the Sunset Celebration.

Freddy was one of those lovable charismatic characters that made Key West lively and quirky and just a damn fun place to live or visit.

Freddy was a fourth-generation conch, and as a young boy was infatuated with flying.

By the time he was 16-years-old, Freddy was a fixture out at the airport on South Roosevelt Drive. He had become a "hangar bum," and washed airplanes in exchange for flying lessons.

Cabanas became a Key West aviation legend and entertained hundreds of thousands of spectators around the world with his dare-devil aerobatics, and he performed stunt flying for the movies, television and commercials.

Freddy Cabanas died in a plane crash on 15 January 2013, along with Mexican television host Jorge Lopez while shooting footage for Lopez's show whose title translates as "Extreme Adrenaline." The site of the crash was a private airstrip on the Mexican island of Cozumel (down there west-southwest of Havana).

Below, please find a few tributes. This says so much about the man:

"Such a tragic loss, Freddie let me fly with him in the Waco towing banners over Key West. Also dropped flowers to a beach-side service for a friend of ours. I feel very honored to

185

have known Fred for the few short years I did. As an ex-Navy pilot we had much to talk about. R.I.P. my friend."

"I'm an M.D. Have flown for many years but went into aerobatic flying because of Fred Cabanas. He gave me my initial lessons and his infectious enthusiasm for aerobatics has always stuck with me. He was a great pilot and an honest ethical human being. God Bless you Freddie. You are deeply missed. Our world needs more people like you, my friend."

"It has been said that Freddy Cabanas, Key West pilot and superhero, turned more people on to flying than all of the US Air Force combined. There was no vehicle on earth he was incapable of flying. If there were a flying car, Fred Cabanas could fly it. Flying carpets were nothing to Freddy Cabanas. Legend has it that kites gravitated towards him but Freddy Cabanas would downplay such suggestions as silliness. (Nonetheless on the day after his death there were no kites flying in Key West.) He had a fondness for good food and company, and with wife, son, daughter and friends and family, Freddy Cabanas was often seen having grand dinners at Mo's Creole Restaurant on White Street. We will miss him but in person only. Freddy Cabanas' spirit now flies up where we belong. Long live Freddy Cabanas! Long Live the Conch Republic Air Force!"

The flags at Key West International Airport were lowered to half-mast in tribute to Freddy's demise.

Cabanas had passed on his love of flying to both his children—his daughter, a Navy pilot, and son who helped his dad fly two planes to Haiti to deliver supplies for orphans after the 2010 earthquake.

Freddy Cabanas was a General in the Conch Republic Air Force.

CHAPTER 89—Will Soto

What can I say about Will Soto?

Lots!

He's Mr. Cool.

He's a Key West icon.

He *is* Sunset Celebration.

He's the king of the hill—"Will's Hill."

He's the type of guy you want on your side when trouble erupts.

Soto was born in Chicago on 13 October (the same birthday as Lenny Bruce), and grew up in leafy Lincoln Park, just a short distance from the Gold Coast, the rich, sandy beaches of Lake Michigan, and the beckoning sports beacon that is Wrigley Field. This was until the age of twelve.

Will's parents then moved out to the burbs, to Rolling Meadows. The Meadows was a new community and had no schools, so Will went to junior high and all of high school (3 different high schools, in fact) in the next community of Arlington Heights.

**AUTHOR'S NOTE: Arlington Heights is home to the world-famous Arlington Park Racecourse.

Okay, folks, you may want to take notes again, as I will now show you how a friendly kid from the suburbs of the Windy City ends up walking on a high wire in Key West, FL, not quite the USA.

First, it helps if you're an athlete, a gymnast to be exact, and you're good enough to have lettered multiple times.

Then you get the itch to see the world, so you join the Navy and do tours in the Baltic, the Caribbean, and the Atlantic.

And you are beguiled by the ocean.

Then fate lends a hand and you stop for liberty in—okay, let's all say it out loud together again—KEY WEST.

And once you've tasted the seductive nectar that the island offers, your life will never be the same.

But Will had aspirations to be an artist (but not a high-wire artist at this point), so after being discharged from the Navy, he enrolled at Southern Illinois University and majored in Art.

After college, Soto gravitated south, first to vibrant Austin for a year, then to historic New Orleans for three years, and he pursued his passion and innate talent, and worked as a sculptor in wood, ivory, antlers, bone, and soft stone. He hit the Festival Circuit throughout the South and Midwest.

And he ended up in Miami, working the Coconut Grove Art Show.

Only 156 miles away from that big gigantic pulsing magnet that is the rock.

When the art show in Coconut Grove was history for another year, an artist friend asked Will if he wanted to come down to Key West to hang out for the winter. Will Soto said he preferred to go back to New Orleans.

The friend said: "Completely understand. Let's have one last drink together."

They did, but the drink was rum and the elixir worked its magical wonders and before Will Soto knew it, he was in the back of a truck "passing over many, many bridges."

Key West was as quaint and quirky as he remembered it and as Will says, "It just felt right."

Will wandered down to Mallory at sunset.

Saw the laidback gathering of gentle folk.

The passing of a bottle.

The passing of a pipe.

There playing of congas.

The Limbo.

And BAM! It all came together and Will Soto knew right then and there that he wanted to stay, HAD to stay, and he knew he could put his God-given talents to work.

He started as a juggler in 1976.

Graduated to the high wire in 1981

**INSIDER ASIDE: I was talking to Will Soto about Key West and his first impressions of the island, and then the subject of Capt. Tony came up, and what Will had to say blew me away.

Here's what Will told me: "Capt. Tony was one of the first people I met when I arrived in Key West. He was the Godfather to all of us 'flower children' (hippies), the Sunset Celebration savior, and Key West Mayor.

He was also my mentor.

I spent many hours at his bar or at Mallory Square. We discussed EVERYTHING from politics to religion, morality, fishing, gambling, smuggling, women, and a few things I can't really mention. Although I love many of his more famous quotes the advice he gave me that I'll always remember the most was: 'Listen to your heart.'

The character trait that most people seem to remember is his womanizing, but the thing I remember the most was how he treated people. It didn't matter to him if you were a visiting prince, a billionaire businessman, a fisherman or a vagrant. Tony treated EVERYONE with the same respect and hospitality. He was constantly feeding and caring for anyone he thought needed it. Whatever he had in this world…he shared with everyone.

In the early 80s, when the City was trying to shut down the Sunset Celebration (mostly because they wanted Mallory for a cruise port), we (the "Sun Setters") were being arrested for imaginary charges. (i.e., "trespassing in a public square," "performing without a permit,"). Capt. Tony would help us to make bail and eventually helped us to organize. We began having rallies ("SOS—Save Our Sunset"), which were community potluck dinners and rallying speeches held at the old Mallory Square Community Center (which eventually became Jan McArt's dinner theater, which is now Maison de Pepes Restaurant & Bar.)

At this time, Tony was already a well-known celebrity/luminary. One day he said to me: "The Sunset Celebration is one of the best things to happen to this town. These guys (politicians) are trying to push you out the back door while no one's watching. Let's turn on the lights and watch the cockroaches run." That said, he called all his contacts he had made in the media, both print and TV, and invited them down.

It was a turning point.

When some of the politician/businessmen (with ulterior motives) were suddenly approached with national media cameras and microphones, they started changing their tune. It took a while, with many lawyers, impassioned speeches and council meetings to save the event...but this was the beginning of the "counter-offensive."

Eventually, as you know, we prevailed and were allowed to lease Mallory Square as the Key West Cultural Preservation Society, the non-profit we established to manage the Sunset Celebration. I consider Capt. Tony both the guardian angel and the godfather of that battle.

Throughout the ensuing years, whether we were at the dog track, playing poker or just kibitzing at his bar, he was always sure to check with me how things were going down at the "Square."

The two men who I love, admire, and respect the most in this world are my father and Capt. Tony.

By the way, did you know that when he was laid out for his wake viewing, he had a pack of Lucky Strikes in one shirt pocket and a deck of cards in the other?

"God, I love that man."

Well said, Will.

* * *

Will Soto is the only remaining founder of the KEY WEST CULTURAL PRESERVATION SOCIETY who's still active.

And now catch this: I don't want to tell you too much more about Will Soto here, because besides being the top act at Sunset and a producer/director of Buskerfest, and a sailor, bon-vivant, smuggler, lover of animals and good jokes, and having Amy to share his life with—Will has become an author.

Yes, you heard right, an AUTHOR.

If you enjoyed that little story above about Capt. Tony, you will love Will's book.

ANOTHER INSIDER NOTE: I've seen extracts from

Will's book, and it's hilarious.

It's inspiring.

It's enlightening.

It will tug at your heartstrings and it will piss you off and it will make you stand up and cheer.

So watch this space, I will be talking about Will's book and its launch date when I get back into my own KEY WEST Book #5 (coming to a Kindle or bookstore near you soon).

* * *

As Will Soto himself says: "If there's a point to be made these days, it's that I'm as happy as I've ever been in my life. That's pretty much my bottom line right now."

Too right.

So, my Dear Reading Amigos, put this down on your dance card: If you've never been down to Mallory Square to catch the Sunset Celebration, go grab a bag of popcorn from Popcorn Joe and then hustle over to the south end of the pier to catch Soto's act.

Be prepared to moon the sunset cruises.

It's a tradition.

If you've already seen Will's show, then go see it again. Simply said, Will Soto is one of the reasons this glorious, magical part of the world exists.

If you want to see how charming and humble Will is, just have a wee snoop at this video where he's being interviewed by Jenna Stauffer.

In a word: Wow!

Okay, two words: Wow and charismatic!

SNOOP HERE, and do it with a drink in your hand—it's Key West! And be sure to SKIP the Ad:

https://www.youtube.com/watch?v=xggNsWb5qHI

CHAPTER 90—Jenna Stauffer

Since we just saw Jenna in action interviewing Will Soto, it is only fitting that we now feature her.

Jenna Stauffer moved to Key West in July of 2010, following her dreams and passion.

And life has never been better.

Jenna has been hosting two TV shows: *Good Morning Florida Keys* and *Key West with Jenna.* The shows offer a plethora of Key West (and Keys) cool stuff in the form of lively interviews with famous celebrities (like Cindy Williams and best-selling crime/thriller author Jeffrey Deaver), and inspirational stories and colorful local personalities and hidden hideaways and back-lane shops and the ins-and-outs of, well, the "in" places to go when you come down to Key West the next time.

PSSST!—if you can keep a secret—Jenna even takes us behind closed doors of idyllic island properties and gives us a sneak-peek of what these coveted homes look like.

CHAPTER 91—Al Subarsky

In Alfonse's own words: "Weened in Belma, N.J., watching Ricky Nelson play guitar at the closing of each *Ozzie and Harriet* episode at the tender age of 12, I decided THIS was for ME, and immediately started learning the instrument on my own.

My cousin Bruce loaned me a guitar, and I was on my way!

Due to a non-scheduled snowball fight on the school bus ride home, I was 45 minutes late for what was to be my one and only formal guitar lesson. Being a one-hour lesson, the teacher (Mr. Flohr) yelled at me, and having Marty Feldman eyes scared the shit out of me! Needless to say, I never had that lesson or any other from that day forward…but it intensified my desire to play…ultimately deciding that jamming with older players would be my education. I never looked back, and have made my living playing guitar for the last 45 years.

The 70s thru the 90s we're very fertile years on the Jersey Shore. There would be 40 to 50 bands playing up and down the tri-state area, before economics, DUI laws, etc., would basically shut the party down. Solo/Duo/Trio work would take over, and when I left the "Party Dolls" band (I provided the guitar for eleven years, '88-'99), I decided to head down to Key West to see if I could find a "place" for myself.

My good friend Colleen Feeney worked at La Concha Hotel during the winter months, and suggested I contact Frank Dudek at the hotel. Frank was assistant manager at the time.

I met with Frank for a half hour in the lobby (it was Holiday Inn, now Crowne Plaza) and never having heard me play or sing, suggested I go back to Jersey, get my gear and start playing four nights a week at "The Top" Rooftop Bar and terrific sunset celebration venue!

My residency would last fifteen years until the powers that be, in their infinite wisdom, decided to shut down "The Top" and build a freakin' health spa! To this day, locals and visitors alike are PISSED OFF about this very bad decision.

But that's the way it goes, my friend!

September 2019 begins my 21st year in the Conch Republic. As I always say, "There are a lot worse places to wake up in the morning."

* * *

Okay, Dear Reader, I'm back and is that a great story from Alfonse, or what?

Remember, and I keep banging away at this, that we only live once. Sometimes we have to jump off the hamster wheel.

Al Subarsky did and boy-oh-boy did he ever land on his flip-flops.

**CUTE FEEL-GOOD NOTE: At Big Al's last gig at The Top of La Concha...everyone came with those large cut-out photographs of a face, you know the ones, they're attached to a stick and you hold it up in front of your face. The face on the photograph was of course Al Subarsky, and there were about 30 or 40 Al Subarskys there that final day.

Will the real Al Subarsky please stand up!

It reminded me of the scene in *E.T.* when Elliot's mother comes back home and thinks something is afoot and looks in the closet and E.T. is in there, big round eyes, hiding among all the stuffed animals.

Cute.

CHAPTER 92—The Key West Island Bookstore

Yes! A bookstore makes the celebrity list.

And it should.

The Key West Island Bookstore is to Key West what Shakespeare and Company was to Paris in the 20s.

Moreover, it offers the parched reader an oasis of books, and it's the focal point of the deeply rooted literary culture on the island.

Suzanne Hughes Orchard, a Pennsylvania native and self-proclaimed "book geek," started working at the bookstore in 2005 as a bookseller, then as manager, and then in 2015 she (along with renowned, top Chef/hubby Paul) was able to buy the bookstore.

The bookstore is a treasure trove of used books, rare books, books by local authors, and books that you just couldn't find anywhere else on the planet.

Suzanne will tell you that her "favorite moments are when she recommends a book by any one of Key West's authors to a snowbird who says, 'I haven't read a book in years, but now I'm on vacation. What should I read?'"

If you are in the hunt for your next book, pop on in the next time you down, meet Suzanne, have a chat about books, she's friendly and extremely knowledgeable…and help support our island's only true independent bookstore.

If you live in the Great White North or further afield, give them a bell and they will happily ship you up just about any book you want, whether it be from local authors, about Key West itself, the latest *New York Times* Bestsellers, all things Hemingway, or even first editions and signed titles. Don't know what you want for that beach read or that cozy armchair read?

They can help!

How about Tom Corcoran, or James W. Hall or David L. Sloan or Carl Hiaasen?

What?

You want to know if they sell rare antiquarian books?

Yes!

What now?

You would like to know what their telephone number is?

I can help you with that: I just happen to have it right here taped to the wall next to where Mr. Leroy sleeps: +1 305-294-2904.

Now what?

You want to know what their address is?

I have that for you, as well: 513 ½ Fleming Street, in Old Town Key West. Look for the "Hemingway plaque" to the right of the front door.

Okay, listen up world!

I'm opening the window and shouting out loud now for all on the streets out there to hear: "**PLEASE SUPPORT YOUR *TRULY* INDEPENDENT BOOKSTORE!**"

Amazon doesn't need the money...

CHAPTER 93—Harry Teaford

Harry Teaford, aka **Harry T**, aka **Billy Ray Flynn**, is in Key West everyday even though he resides in Islamorada. No, he doesn't have a life-sucking commute…

Harry T is on the radio!

Harry T is the Founder, Owner and Radio Host of A1A Media: "Radio A1A," "Cruisin' Country Radio" and "Paradise Road Radio."

If you haven't heard, may I just mention that the mighty Radio A1A received the coveted 2016 & 2017 Trop Rock Music Association "Radio Station of the Year Award."

That's heady stuff!

How did Harry T end up here in the Keys, on our car radios, in our homes, on our boats? you ask.

For Harry, it all started in Mobile, AL, which is a helluva glorious place to start.

Have you ever been to Mobile?

Have seen Historic Downtown? It's quaint and it's exceedingly picturesque.

**FY-Mobile-I: I spent many winters in Mobile on my grandparent's farm when I was growing up, and I've never forgotten those cherished years, the laid-back ambience, the southern charm.

Anyhoo, back to Harry. He's always been "all about music and all about show business."

And he's blessed with a strong, mellifluous voice.

In 1971, as a high school student, he was "Allstate Tenor" as part of the highly regarded Alabama State Chorus.

See?

In 1975, after graduating from the University of Mobile in Gulf Shores, AL., Harry began his musical career in earnest as lead singer and bass player for the variety band "Family" at the Gulf State Convention Center Lounge.

I told you he had a great voice.

Still with Family, he gigged to rave reviews at the Biloxi Hilton and The Tiki in Gautier, MS.

Have you ever been to the Biloxi Hilton?

The Tiki?

Famed venues.

Posh venues.

The man sang and entertained all along the Gulf Coast aka the "Redneck Riviera," making quite a name for himself and developing a loyal following.

This led to him joining the popular group "Jubilation." This ended up being a win-win for all, as Harry Teaford toured with them for over 30 years, eventually becoming the leader of Jubilation and musical director for shows featuring Percy Sledge, Bobby Purify, The Platters, Ace Cannon, the Drifters, the Coasters and many more well-known recording artists.

About now I'm mumbling *Holy shit!* because I'm well-impressed, I have to tell you.

Jubilation evolved and changed names becoming the "Blue Eyed Soul Brothers," which is a kinda cool name and really says it all about their style.

If I had been there I would no doubt have thrown my shoe up at the stage as a show of respect.

The Blue Eyed Soul Brothers went on to even greater success and played in front of packed to the gills venues throughout the entire Southeastern United States.

In 1990, Harry worked as well with the "Dixie Mules" rhythm & blues band of all-star musicians of members of other famous groups in the southeast.

Sort of his era Traveling Wilburys, if you will.

And then: DRUM ROLL, PLEASE.

Radio called.

And remember he had "that mellifluous voice."

In 1994, he began his career as the popular radio talk show host of "Braggin' Rights" sports radio, broadcasting out of Mobile. Later Harry hosted the "Inside The Saints" radio show on WNSP and the New Orleans Saints Network. Since Harry was and is an avid Alabama Crimson Tide fan he hosted the shows under the stage name "Billy Ray Flynn."

So THAT'S where his *nom de plume* came from!

And then the Florida Keys called and this was good news for all of us. Mobile's loss was our gain.

He created and hosted the "Money Wize" Radio Show, WORZ FM Ocean Reef, Florida Keys.

In 2012 Harry created an internet radio station called "Radio A1A" and then in March of 2013, launched the Radio A1A 24/7 broadcast of "Trop Rock" music entertainment and information. What that means is, Harry was the pioneer of the musical genre known as Trop Rock.

If you haven't ever followed Harry T on the radio, you can do it right here. As aforementioned, he teams up with Mayor Gonzo Mays.

He's the yin to Mayor Gonzo Mays' yang.

A dynamic duo.

Cheeky, enlightening and hilarious.

https://radioa1a.com/the-weekly-trop-40/

AUTHOR'S NOTE: I've given you this background on Harry T/Billy Ray, because I find it inordinately interesting how folk from yonder parts are drawn to the Keys and Key West.

Their journeys fascinate me.

Sometimes their routes are circuitous, sometimes they are long, arduous even.

Getting here is what's important, not how you come or which road (or sea), just that you do, indeed, get your derrière here.

CHAPTER 94—Cindy Williams

Yes, that Cindy Williams.

"Shirley Feeney" of *Laverne* & *Shirley* fame.

Cindy Williams was born August 22, 1947, in Van Nuys, CA, that's in the San Fernando Valley, just over the Hollywood Hills (and Santa Monica Mountains) from L.A.

One of Cindy's classmates was actress Sally Field.

Do you remember Cindy Williams played Ron Howard's high school sweetheart in George Lucas' 1973 coming-of-age film *American Graffiti?*

Love that movie.

**AUTHOR'S CELLULOID NOTE: Did *American Graffiti* have enough future stars in it, or what?

Richard Dreyfuss
Harrison Ford
Ron Howard
Cindy Williams
Charles Martin Smith
Suzanne Somers
Joe Spano
Mackenzie Phillips
Kay Lentz
Bo Hopkins
Kathleen Quinlan
And Wolfman Jack

Anyhoo, that aside, Cindy Williams was the Grand Marshal of the Key West Fantasy Fest Parade in 2015.

She had never been to Key West before and LOVED IT down here!

Here's another great interview with Jenna Stauffer and the adorable and hilarious Cindy Williams:

https://www.youtube.com/watch?v=VX-AQr6gss8

* * *

And now EVERYONE UP ON YOUR FEET!
That's it!
And now sing along with me:

**"One-two-three-four-
five-six-seven-eight,
Schlemiel, Schlimazel,
Hasenpfeffer Incorporated…"**

CHAPTER 95—Penny Leto

Penny Leto is the owner of the CoffeeMill Dance Studio, and there are now TWO locations: one at 804 White Street in the Old Town (two separate studios here) and another studio "By the Bay" out on North Roosevelt in the New Town.

Sounds appealing, doesn't it?

Penny was one of the original members of the Spectrelles ("Toni Spectrelle"). Do you remember her? Dark, burning good looks? Yes, that's her.

Gabrielle and I used to go watch her at The Bull, as well.

Now we take Zumba from her.

Penny was born and raised in the Bronx and headed down to Key West in 1977 with a B.A. in Dance Education from Herbert H. Lehman College.

When the old CoffeeMill property came up for sale in 1984, Penny pounced, purchased it, and then co-founded the Key West Dance Theatre.

Penny choreographs for all the theatre groups in Key West including Keys Kids, the Waterfront Playhouse, and the Red Barn Theatre, and produces DanceWorks! (this year featured *A Midsummer's Night Dream*).

FY-*arabesque*-I: Penny Leto is a one-woman culture-creating machine.

FY-keep-fit-I: The DanceMill offers classes for EVERYONE, from beginners to pre-professionals. Even for kids 3 years and up. All ages and all skill levels.

Have you ever wanted to take a Pole Dance class? You can do it here. And it's a great way to keep fit!

How about Zumba or Tap or Ballet or Contemporary or Pointe or Modern or Jazz or Lyrical or African Dance or

Capoeira (an Afro-Brazilian martial art that combines elements of dance, acrobatics, and music)?

They have it all.

What's that you ask? *They wouldn't happen to offer Aerial Yoga, would they?*

Well, yes, they do offer Aerial Yoga, and I'm glad you asked. Now what?

Do they offer Hip Hop?

Yes (and Hippity Hop for the little ones).

And before you ask, I will just say a big YES to Bellydance. How 'bout that!

TOP MARKS NOTE: The CoffeeMill Dance Studio was named "Best Dance Studio in Florida" by Florida Monthly Magazine.

What are you waiting for?

Come on over.

Check it out.

CHAPTER 96—Duane "Bongo D" Scott

Gabrielle and I first met Duane when he performed down at the pier in the early 1990s. Duane is one of those individuals who came to Key West, fell in love with the island and embraced its spirit.

Bongo D is an accomplished musician. If you're planning on getting married in Key West, you might want to hire Bongo D to come and play the steel drum to give "that special day" the flavor of the islands.

Ask him to blow the conch shell for you.

CHAPTER 97—David L. Sloan

The man is funny.

And he's scary.

And he's informative.

Listen up:

He's an author (books: funny, scary, and informative).

An historian.

An inventor.

An entrepreneur.

A chef.

A leading authority on Key lime pie.

A publisher "Phantom Press" (books: funny, scary, and informative).

Shall I go on?

He's the co-producer of the Cow Key Channel Bridge Run (the world's first "ZERO-K," a tongue-in-cheek, no bull, bovine-themed alternative to the demanding 7-Mile Bridge Run). *If you can make it to the start, you can make it to the finish.*

He's a co-founder of The Key Lime Festival (an orgasmic event and not to be missed).

A co-founder of the "One Seed at a Time" initiative to replant Key lime trees and repopulate suitable land of the Lower Keys with real Key limes.

He's also "Ghost Hunts & Haunted Tours in Key West."

Have a peek at **HAUNTED KEY WEST TOURS** (SLOAN'S KEY WEST GHOST HUNT TOUR), but be very, very afraid:

https://hauntedkeywest.com/activities/sloans-key-west-ghost-hunt/

David Sloan is a shining example of what can be done if you leave the real world behind and strike out in the direction of new horizons.

You just might find talents that you never even knew you had along the way.

I was going to say that David has his fingers in a lot of pies, ah, Key lime pies, but I won't as that would generate another groan from you.

How can you not like a fellow who says this: "I first visited Key West in college, and even though I spent most of the night sobering up in a jail cell, I loved it!"

AUTHOR'S NOTE: This is the type of pedigree that will serve you well if you are thinking of quitting your job and moving to Key West.

Wait! That's the title of one of his bestselling books (with Christopher Shultz): *QUIT YOUR JOB AND MOVE TO KEY WEST.*

The book's hilarious and it will light a fire under your ass, which is exactly what I venture to say you need in your life right now.

Get David L. Sloan's book. (Don't forget the middle initial "L" when ordering.)

Study it.

Then sell up.

David L. Sloan has written over twenty books, so you'll have a veritable galaxy of "Summer Beach Reads" when you move down where it's pretty much summer all year round.

And this from the man himself: "I love Key West because it has that small town feel with big city benefits. It really is easy to succeed here if you put yourself out there and get to know the kind of person you are.

"This community rallies around you and helps you to succeed, and that's why I'm here today. There really is no place in the United States like it."

CHAPTER 98—Sallie Foster

Sallie can often be found at The Bull, tickling the piano, ripping on her electric guitar, and generally blowing the roof off (which is not easy to do, what with the Whistle Bar and the Garden of Eden Rooftop Bar up above).

Sallie can warble all known songs, has a cracking portfolio of her own originals, and revels in getting tourists up on stage to perform as her back-up dancers.

WARNING #1: Don't attempt being a back-up dancer unless you're suitably hammered and your blood alcohol level is above .08.

WARNING #2: As back-up dancers you just might be cajoled to do something rude, which, let's face it, it's one of the reasons you popped down to Key West in the first place.

WARNING #3: Sallie just loves to roam the bar while she's singing and playing the guitar, and she just might follow you to the toilet STILL SINGING AND PLAYING.

So no riding the porcelain bus.

And no naughties!

CHAPTER 99—Nick Norman

The man with the affable grin.

The man with the infectious smile.

Nick Norman has become one of Key West's top draws ever since he said goodbye to South Carolina and made his way down Highway #1.

"I came down here to see **Joal Rush** at the Hog's Breath and got up and played a few tunes with him, and we walked over to the Lazy Gecko and Irish Kevin's, and I played there."

That had not been planned. Norman had only made the trip to Key West to chill out a bit.

By the end of his first night, he already had job offers.

It was a classic no-brainer.

Norman went back up to South Carolina, sold his pawn shop and income tax service and hightailed it right back down to the rock.

He was home before he even got here.

Key West is a music town.

A damn good one.

Now he gets to play music on his terms, doesn't have to be away from his daughter and wife.

He's living the dream.

Cool.

BTW: Norman's wife landed on her artistic feet here, as well, she's Kelly Norman, the Director of the Key West Theater, over at 512 Eaton Street.

Nick Norman is the Creative Director.

Cool, again.

CHAPTER 100—The Cookie Lady

Do you remember The Cookie Lady?

Marilyn Kellner came to Key West in the 80s and was one of the founding members of the Key West Cultural Preservation Society (along with Will Soto), the umbrella of the mega-popular and iconic Sunset Celebration.

At Sunset, Marilyn would straddle her bicycle, tippy-toe along through the thong-wearing throngs, recite her poetry, and sell killer brownies and orgasmic cookies to the "hungry hungry," in-need-of-munchies folk who came to worship the sun squatting on the distant horizon.

As The Cookie Lady told me (in her inimitable poetic fashion):

> **I set sail for Key West from Lake Erie,**
> **Though I had no time on the Ocean,**
> **I was not worried or leery.**
> **Life in forward motion!**
> **On the 6-week sail down,**
> **thinking what I could do in this town.**
> **As genes from my mom as a home baker,**
> **Acquired as well as her talent as rhyme-maker.**
> **So all came together at Mallory Pier,**
> **On my bicycle I yelled rhymes all could hear.**
> **And made original baked goods to "pedal"**
> **Key West, my heaven, where I settle.**
> **When peddling no more,**
> **So many still did adore.**
> **So as an artist I entirely published a book,**
> **Filled with some of "Rhymes and Recipes".**

And a book she has out INDEED...which you can find at the Key West Island Bookstore to READ.

Pop in when you're next on the island and ask for "RHYMES & RECIPES" by The Cookie Lady of Key West, Marilyn Kellner.

It's a mouth-watering good read.

CHAPTER 101—Gary Hempsey

This speaks volumes: **"Gary Hempsey is the only non-country act to open for Kenny Chesney."**

And if you see him perform, you'll know why.

Gary plays adult acoustic alternative, from soft acoustic to cutting edge, and he's known for putting his own spin on the music of the legends from Buffett to The Beatles.

If you are in the hunt for one helluva memorable evening, look for him at Boondocks, the Schooner Wharf, and the Galleon Sunset Tiki.

See if you can catch him when he's doing his thing with his amigo **Terry Cassidy**.

The following is from his appearance at this year's Earth Day (I'm including this because it really sums up Gary Hempsey):

"Help us celebrate Earth Day with a fugitive band of hippies from the 1960s that have been hiding out and performing in Key West. They all used to have long hair, smoke weed, and could play any song anyone could remember from the 60s. The band motto is 'If someone knows part of a song, we'll follow them to the gates of hell.'

"Band Leader Gary Hempsey and That Hippie Band will help you remember all those songs from the Age of Aquarius. Plenty of old favorites from the Grateful Dead, The Beatles, Rolling Stones, Jefferson Starship, maybe even some Crosby, Stills & Nash will be rediscovered."

CHAPTER 102—Popcorn Joe

Joe Bement was living in Virginia Beach and drove down to Key West with a group of Native Tan Suntan Lotion distributors in June of 1983.

This would have been a fun job back then, I'm thinking, what with hitting all the sunny, palm-lined beach cities as part of your job description.

Giuseppe (as Gabrielle and I call him) liked Key West so much, he flew right back down that December.

He stayed at the Spanish Gardens Motel on the corner of Simonton and South Street.

It was the 29th of December and Joe took a stroll down Duval and past the old Cuban Club. He stopped to take a photo and then decided to head over to Capt. Tony's for a cool one.

Oddly, it was unseasonably cold for Key West that night with the temperature in the forties (that's not what he was expecting when he had designs on a cool one). When Popcorn Joe entered Capt. Tony's, he found Tony in there burning "beer flats" in the fireplace to keep warm.

In the distance, they could hear sirens and both joked, hoping it was not on account of their roaring fire.

Popcorn Joe and Capt. Tony hit it right off and ended up becoming life-long friends.

On the way back to his hotel, Joe approached the old Cuban Club again and was shocked to find it burning to the ground.

In 1984, Popcorn Joe purchased three houses that would become the Pineapple Apartments complex and spent a hunk of time renovating his own apartment there, putting on a large 2nd-floor deck out back, adding a swimming pool and gradually turning the two other houses into six rental units.

The man is a master at restoration.

The Pineapple Apartments is where Gabrielle and I worked when we first arrived in Key West in 1991.

We lived in the attic above Popcorn Joe's apartment.

It was hot and stuffy up there, it was cramped, there was no storage, the commode was out in the middle of what functioned as our living room, there was no kitchen sink, the refrigerator was the size of a pet carrier, and we had to bend over a lot.

And we felt we were the luckiest people in the world.

We had a roof over our heads in Key West, FL, not quite the USA.

And we had jobs.

Before Popcorn Joe started flogging popcorn down at "Sunset" (and became "Popcorn Joe"), he needed some extra income while he was renovating the Pineapple Apartments, so in his spare time, he solicited time shares on the street for the Gallon Resort.

You gotta do what you gotta do.

So there you go, a little background info on one helluva nice guy.

**BTW: Popcorn Joe Bement has risen to the rank of local celebrity by simply appearing in so many damn books.

CHAPTER 103—Fats Navarro

Theodore "Fats" Navarro was born in Key West in 1923, of Cuban-Black-Chinese parentage. He grew up in Bahama Village at 828 Thomas Street. (Bike on over there.)

His mother, Miriam (Navarro) Williams, was the cook for Ernest and Pauline Hemingway, and she was there when Hemingway started cheating on Pauline with the blond, leggy journalist Martha Gellhorn.

Miriam recalls seeing Hemingway and Gellhorn out in the garden, together, alone, canoodling:

"There would be parties and Mr. Ernest and Miss Martha would be outside kissing and carrying on…the way some people act!"

* * *

Fats Navarro began playing piano at age six, but didn't become serious about music until taking up the trumpet at 12 or 13. After graduating from Frederick Douglass High School in Key West's Bahama Village, and eager to see the world, he joined a dance band and headed north.

As a trumpet player, Fats Navarro was a pioneer of the bebop style of jazz improvisation in the 1940s. He played with Charlie Parker, Benny Goodman, and Lionel Hampton. He is ranked with Dizzy Gillespie and Miles Davis as one of the most gifted and original stylists in the development of jazz.

Theodore "Fats" Navarro died in New York City, at the young age of 26 of a heroin overdose.

Six days before his untimely death, he gave a memorable performance with his friend Charlie Parker at the landmark jazz club "Birdland" in the jazz Mecca of New York City, where shows began at 9pm and went on until dawn.

Fats Navarro may have quit Key West, but Key West will

never forget him.

SCHOOL NOTE: Frederick Douglass High School was the school the island's black students attended when the Monroe County schools were segregated.

It ceased being segregated in 1965.

HISTORICAL NOTE: Frederick Douglass was an abolitionist, orator, writer, and statesman. He escaped from slavery in Maryland and became a national leader of the abolitionist movement.

CHAPTER 104—Coffee Butler

Lofton "Coffee" Butler was born in Key West, raised in Key West, and attended Frederick Douglass High School in Bahama Village, as well.

Family and friends used to call him Loffy except for one friend who kept mispronouncing Loffy and it came out as "Coffee."

"Coffee" was cool, "Loffy" not so, so Coffee it was.

In high school, Coffee showed immense musical talent and was encouraged by his music teacher, a lovely lady by the name of Miss Ellen Sanchez.

Coffee's father was a musician, as well, and even though Coffee was still in school, they formed a band together and used to play the Imperial Café, the Cuban Club, and the old Bamboo Room on what is now Applerouth Lane.

One particular night, Tennessee Williams came in to the Bamboo Room with the fiery actress Tallulah Bankhead hanging on his arm. After listening to Coffee sing and play the piano, Tallulah rose, slinked up to Coffee, and sat on his piano. The young and handsome Coffee Butler gushed and told Tallulah how he loved her movies and her deep sexy voice.

Tallulah Bankhead eyed the young man, gave him the once over, and quipped: "If you made love to me, you would have been dead a long time ago."

SPORTY NOTE: Coffee Butler was an outstanding shortstop and his idol was Jackie Robinson. Coffee was keen to follow in the cleated footsteps of Jackie Robinson, so after graduation from high school in 1948, he put his music career on hold and tried out with the Negro League's Kansas City Monarchs and ended up playing in the Florida/Cuba League from 1950 to 1951 for the Palm Beach Rockets. With the

Rockets, Coffee traveled to away games up in Miami and Tampa, and even down to Cuba.

In 1952, Coffee Butler was drafted into military service.

After serving his country, Coffee returned to Key West and playing music.

Local fame came and word spread and Coffee had an offer to go out to Las Vegas for a bigger stage, bigger crowds and more money.

But he opted to stay in Key West. Key West was his home, he had married the love of his life—and he remembered what had happened to his dear friend Fats Navarro.

When Harry Truman was down in Key West for the dedication of Truman Avenue, Coffee Butler sang "The Beautiful Isle of Key West" for the then president. The song was written by Ellen Sanchez, yes, the one and only—Coffee's high school music teacher.

What? What did you want to know?

Well, yes, I do just happen to have Coffee Butler singing that age-old song right here, following the obligatory Ad:

https://www.youtube.com/watch?v=aH8MYJ3bHYE

As of this printing, Coffee Butler is just celebrating his 91st birthday.

And may you have many, many more Coffee Butler!

CHAPTER 105—Cliff Sawyer

In a similar track to Coffee Butler, Sawyer was born, raised and, for the most part, stayed tethered to the rock. Cliff sang in the church choir and graduated from Key West High School in 1966, merely a year after the high school had become desegregated.

"Corner bands" were extremely popular and as a little boy Sawyer enjoyed listening to the sounds of the street from his bedroom window in Bahama Village.

When Gabrielle and I lived in Aronovitz Lane, we would come home late from selling our Sunset Photos down at Mallory Square and see Cliff Sawyer in the Green Parrot singing "Love Train." It would be hot and steamy and folk would park their bicycles out front and if the place was jammed inside (which it usually was), folk would just sit out front on the sidewalk on chairs or chaise lounges they'd brought from home.

It was a great scene.

And a wonderful way to spend an evening.

Here's Cliff Sawyer singing at the Green Parrot "chicken and waffle gospel brunch"

https://www.youtube.com/watch?v=QVP7b5kYguA

Perhaps a bit more appreciation of the legend that is Cliff Sawyer would have been nice and less stuffing of the faces.

CHAPTER 106—Barry Cuda

For those of you who don't know who Barry Cuda is, I will just mention that he's a local singer/pianist who's adopted the stress-free method of pushing his upright piano through the streets of Old Town Key West, from gig to gig, to avoid worrying about if he'll be able to find a place to park a van.

He even makes "house calls" as he did tickling the keys and singing the bluesy "Saint James Infirmary" outdoors at the Key West Cemetery.

Here's the start of the song:

**I WENT DOWN TO THE KEY WEST CEMETERY
DOWN OLD TOWN BY THE MALLORY SQUARE
SEVEN GHOSTS AS USUAL
AND A FEW ROOSTERS ALSO WERE THERE
I WENT UP TO SEE MY BABY
MISS MARGARET'S HER NAME
SHE WAS STRETCHED OUT ON A COOL
TOMBSTONE
SINGING THE SAME OL' SAME
I WENT DOWN TO THE GREEN PARROT
SAW MY BUDDIES THERE
THEY WERE SERVING DRINKS AS USUAL
AND ALL MY GOOD BUDDY BARFLIES WERE
HERE...**

This was a touching tribute to a beloved one departed by the name of Margaret Fryer. Only in Key West would someone of the ilk of Barry Cuda be requested to push his piano up gently sloping Solares Hill to pay homage to a loved one laid to rest.

If you would have liked to have been a fly on a palm tree that sunny, sad afternoon, here it is right in front of you:
https://www.youtube.com/watch?v=_oEtczZZiAw

Now…as Barry Cuda himself will tell you: "I've been gigging at Sloppy's coming up on 30 years this January. I guess I've become a bit of the resident historian, musically. I've been at the Hog's Breath off and on since it came into being in the late 80s.

"All my band buddies love the ambiance of B.O.'s Fish Wagon. It's funky chic. The audience there is not the typical cattle found on Duval. Chances are that if you are curious enough to move away from the 'strip' to see something unique, you'll be open-minded enough to dig some music that is a little off the beaten path, as well."

Yeehah!

Barry Cuda also loves playing the Green Parrot and considers it "the most interesting bar musically on the island, and in South Florida for that matter."

**YOUR ASSIGNMENT: Go to the Green Parrot, get appropriately wasted, and see if you can find the portrait of Barry Cuda "eating the musical notes off the spoon in the painting on the stage."

It's just right there in your grill.

CHAPTER 107—Tom Luna

Question #1: How many people do you know who have a passion for both motorcycles and ballet?

Question #2: How many people do you know who grew up in Mobile, AL, and have a passion for both motorcycles and ballet?

Just as I thought.

"I studied at Tidewater Ballet in Virginia, and then at the American Ballet Theater in New York City," Tom says. "I danced ballet for years, but I couldn't be funny or sing, and I wanted to entertain and make people laugh and that doesn't often happen on the ballet stage."

But it does here in Key West…the being funny and singing and entertaining and making people laugh.

The Key West Citizen had this to say about Tom Luna: "He sings, he dances, he acts, and he makes a mean Key lime martini—often all at the same time."

What?

Where?

When?

If you like a good time, and presumably you do because you're down here, or planning to, ah, get down soon, then you might just want to hump that canny little behind of yours over to the new, fab Marker Resort at 200 William Street, located right there by the waterfront.

**YOUR ASSIGNMENT: Slink over to the huge Wyland mural, ogle it for a bit, take it all in, then swivel around and look right behind you. You are standing in front of The Marker.

So this is where Tom Luna plies his trade and works his magic behind the bar. If you want to have a pop or three and you want to laugh and glow (and not just from the Key lime martini), and you want to meet one of our true Key West characters, this is the place to be.

Hang with Tom.

Tuesdays through Saturdays "sometimes from 10am until 3pm and sometimes from 3 to 10pm," he says. "My scheduled shift varies."

Remember, in Key West, locals don't go to bars, they go to bartenders.

Alternatively, for those who prefer the other side of the coin, slip on over to "Aqua" at 711 Duval and be prepared to be amazed with Tom Luna appearing in "Dueling Bartenders" on Monday nights, 5pm till 8pm, where Tom, along with fellow bartenders and local celebrity musicians, sing show-tunes and theme songs.

It's also two-for-one happy hour, so you might as well get three sheets to the prevailing Westerlies.

YOWZAA! NOTE: Aqua won the 2019 "Bubba Award" for the best gay bar in Key West, and 4th time in a row, mind you.

So what else do you want to know about Tom Luna?

How about how multi-talented he is? He's an actor, director, singer, compere, fundraiser, activist, yes a biker (he tools around the island on his purple 2003 Yamaha Roadster), ballet dancer and…an all-around good chap.

His theatrical credits include, and this is just here in Key West: "Lend Me a Tenor", "I Hate Hamlet", "Little Shop of Horrors", "Forum, Lips Together Teeth Apart" and "Talley's Folly." With his acting-partner-in-crime Danny Weathers, Tom starred in "The Big Bang", "The Mystery of Irma Vep" and "The Complete Works of William Shakespeare, abridged."

And, as noted above, he directs and he did just that for: "Sordid Lives" at the Red Barn Theater, and he directed and acted in "When Pigs Fly" and Howard Crabtree's "Whoop-Dee-Doo." He has sung with the Key West Pops, emceed for various organizations, does concert appearances and was an original member of the Flamingo Follies.

Fantasy Fest just gone, Tom entertained at the famous Headdress Ball, and also emceed the Mayor's Ball in January.

And I know you're wondering, so let me put you out of

your mind, I mean misery, by answering Yes! Tom Luna was even Fantasy Fest King once upon a time in the Conch Republic.

BREAKING NEWS: Tom Luna has just won the coveted 2019 Bubba Award for "**Best Thespian or Performing Artist.**"
Well done Tom!

CHAPTER 108—Caffeine Carl

Caffeine Carl Wagoner is a Conch, born and raised right here in Key West.

Once upon a time, he toured as a member of The Nick Norman Band, but now prefers to stay home and gig locally.

Have you ever seen him shred guitar? In 2015, he was voted the Bubba Award winner for **Best Musician in Key West**.

That says a lot.

Caffeine Carl is a tall, impressive gentle-giant who plays directly from the heart, and has long been inspired by the likes of Eric Clapton and the legendary blues guitarist Albert King.

And it shows.

If you are down here in Cayo Hueso, look out for Caffeine Carl (and The Buzz) at Smokin' Tuna, or over at the Lazy Gecko playing with Tony Baltimore and Lee Venters.

Savage.

CHAPTER 109—Robert Albury

Like Coffee Butler and Cliff Sawyer, Robert Albury is a true Conch and the "King of Key West soul." Albury grew up on the fringe of Bahama Village, on Amelia where it meets Whitehead Street.

Jump on your bicycle again and pedal on over to the Coral City Elks Club on Whitehead near Amelia. That used to be a nightclub where Louis Armstrong would play in the 1950s.

As a boy, Robert Albury would sneak out a bedroom window, climb up on the roof, and revel in the voice and sound of Louis Armstrong as he performed down below on the open-air stage out back. These nights had a powerful and long-lasting influence on the young boy, and it was at this time he knew what he wanted to do for the rest of his life.

And he has.

Robert Albury can often be spotted riding around the Old Town on his bike singing aloud and that I do believe adds to the charm and ambience of Key West.

And he can be found performing down at the foot of Duval at the Sunset Pier at sunset, as well.

He's soul and passion at its utmost best!

CHAPTER 110—Harry Powell

Harry was a City Commissioner.

He also was the Pier Manager down at Mallory when Gabrielle and I were selling our Sunset Photos on the pier.

And he was our neighbor when we lived in Aronovitz Lane (He lived just around the corner on Whitehead near the Green Parrot).

Harry Powell was deeply bothered by the rampant gentrification and the rape of paradise by rapacious developers. And he was especially bothered by the construction of "unnecessary Naval housing" on the undeveloped leafy green at Peary Court, over there at the confluence of White Street and Palm Avenue. The area had long been used by local families as a park to enjoy.

Unlike just about everyone else, Harry decided to do something about it. In January of 1994, he strapped explosives to his chest, grabbed a can of gasoline and what looked to be blasting caps, and barricaded himself in a construction trailer on the Navy property.

Workers ran for their lives.

Harry phoned the police and started negotiating: "This is Harry Powell, former City Commissioner. I have taken over Perry Court construction site. I have explosives…"

Harry demands were clear: He wanted the big brass up in Washington to review the inanity of building Naval Housing here while they tore it down elsewhere.

After an all-day standoff, Harry was promised that his demands would be met and all issues would be reviewed.

Harry surrendered, was immediately arrested, denied bond, tried, and spent nearly a year in prison.

And construction at Peary Court went on without so much as a hitch.

CHAPTER 111—Randy Roberts

First off, Randy Roberts is intelligent.

And talented.

And hilarious.

And extremely likeable.

And sings live, not lip-syncs.

Randy, who comes off just a bit naughty on stage and, well, randy, first hit the boards doing repertory in high school.

When Randy was studying "Theatre Craft," he and his acting classmates decided to get dressed up, as one does, for *The Rocky Horror Picture Show*.

Randy got dressed up in full drag and his friends were absolutely blown away by how gorgeous he was, AND THOSE LEGS! so he started entering contests and doing shows and clubs and, as he told a friend back then: "I can do better than that!"

And he could.

And he did.

And he auditioned the next week and got hired.

Now Randy Roberts can be found entertaining at LaTeDa, dazzling crowds with his impersonations of Bette Midler and Cher and Joan Rivers and Mae West and Joan Crawford and Phyllis Diller and Carol Channing, plus a repertoire of original characters, including "Consuela"—The Latin Showgirl.

"I would do Streisand, but I can't get her voice down, it's a unique instrument, and I would do Celine, but I would be too bruised from hitting my chest."

Gotta love him.

And as Randy says: "I always wanted to be on stage…I'm a female impersonator, I'm an actor who has made his living impersonating other people."

And right he is.

**Bi-TW: Randy Roberts is bi-... Bi-lingual, that is, and he performs at clubs in Puerto Rico and Spain.

People! GRAB everyone you know and get your skates on and cruise on up to LaTeDa on the gay end of Duval, enjoy the show and be prepared to be, well, outrageously IMPRESSED.

CHAPTER 112—Sushi

As a once connoisseur and judge of local chicken of the sea, Sushi (now married) has grown in to a proper Key West legend.

Sushi is in fact one Gary Marion who entertains nightly on the 2nd floor of the world-renowned 801 Bourbon Bar.

If you've been living in a deep, dark cave with a lousy internet signal, let me be the first to tell you that Gary is a drag queen.

The grande dame of drag queens, might I add.

Let's take a quick step back in time:

In 1994, Gary Marion was living in Portland, Oregon, and it wasn't so much that he needed to jump off the hamster wheel as he needed a fresh start with a new lover.

See?

Did you catch that?

It doesn't matter what gets you down here, what's important is simply taking the life-changing plunge.

Nobody says once you get here that you have to work at Strunk's Hardware or the DMV. There's loads of opportunity here for every person of every size and shape and persuasion and ilk.

This is Gary talking to *Keys Voices*: "Of course I'd heard all about the rich LGBTQ history of Key West and all the famous gays that had made it their home or vacation spot.

"From the moment I arrived, it was an instant love story. I was head over heels, literally. There was then, as there is today, a fabulous, quirky local scene of artists and eccentrics that are welcoming and supportive.

"Back then, there existed a tight-knit drag community, but there was no established drag cabaret. I saw an opportunity—a place for me to spread my wings and make a life and home."

See?

229

In 1996, the owner of Bourbon St., Joey Schroeder, and the then manager Jimmy Gilleran (who now owns 801), had a crazy idea to celebrate New Year's Eve, and they told their plans to Sushi: "Let's do a shoe drop. It'll be like the ball drop in Times Square. You'll come down in a giant high-heeled red shoe and we'll ring in the New Year."

So they did.

Word spread faster than the Great Fire of Key West in 1886, and hundreds upon hundreds of folk came to cheer and sing and celebrate.

And the police freaked and tried to close it all down because the owner didn't have a permit.

"The police came upstairs to the balcony and told me to get out of the shoe," Sushi said. "The owner called the mayor and the mayor was like, 'Just let Sushi sit in the shoe. Close down the street.'"

Today, the New Year's Eve "shoe drop" still stars Sushi and folk come from all over the world to take part in the revelry.

The Bourbon St. Pub festivities were once the place for the gay community to ring in the New Year.

Today, the crowd is a glorious mix.

And Gary Marion/Sushi will tell you: "You'll have older gay men next to a family with kids, next to guys in leather, next to a bunch of rowdy bachelorettes. Everybody's welcome in Key West."

**AUTHOR'S OMG NOTE: Gary/Sushi is a fantastic Costume Designer, having worked at the Red Barn Theatre, The Waterfront Playhouse, and the Tennessee Williams Theatre.

Sushi is also a fantastic cook and just as fantastic car mechanic.

If the shoe fits wear it.

It's Key West.

CHAPTER 113—Christopher Peterson

Christopher Peterson grew up in Canada and played the lead role in *Oliver* in school at the age of eleven and was so outstanding, he was chosen to tour with a professional cast of *Oliver*.

He won a Dora, the equivalent of Broadway's Tony Award, for a role as a young man dying of AIDS in the play *Poor Superman*.

"I died 1,600 times, eight times a week," he says.

**AUTHOR'S THESPIAN NOTE: It has to be good for the soul when you're such a competent actor that you can die on stage and still be a hit.

Now Christopher is a headliner at the Cabaret Bar in LaTeDa during the winter high season (along with Randy Roberts).

Christopher is famous for his spooky-good impersonations of Joan Rivers, Marilyn Monroe, Judy Garland…and keeping it in the family, he does a screamer of a Liza Minnelli.

Christopher Peterson spends summers in Rehoboth Beach, Delaware, and winters in Key West.

"Rehoboth and Key West, both in high season. I love Rehoboth and Rehoboth loves me," he says, "but Key West is home."

CHAPTER 114—Howard Livingston

Howard Livingston fled the cold and rat race of the corporate world in the Great White North when he was in his mid-50s, moved to the laidback Keys and embraced his life-long fantasy—music.

"It was an act of freedom," Livingston says. "I decided, I'm going to go down there in flip-flops and T-shirts and see what happens."

And it happened big time.

Livingston started his own band, the Mile Marker 24 Band. The band's style of music is basically "Trop Rock," a mix of rock, reggae and other Caribbean strains.

Livingston and his band have recorded six albums and have become a regular act at festivals and charity events.

Just another example what you can do if you are willing to take the leap (with a guitar strapped to your back).

And NEVER think that you're too old to make the leap: 50s, 60s, 70s, 80s, 90s…it's your life.

CHAPTER 115—Liz O'Connor

Okay, all you Dear Readers, are you thinking of taking the leap like I just talked about above and coming on down to Key West to start a new life?

Thought so.

Liz O'Connor had the guts to do it, and here's how she turned a dream into reality and made it all happen:

"I first discovered the magic of Key West in 1996, when my husband and I vacationed here. I had heard of the island, but had no idea of how special it really was. I had lived in upstate New York my entire life and had spent most vacations at seaside resorts and felt most alive by the ocean. My dream had always been to someday live in a warm place by the ocean, and play music full time. I had been working as a musician part-time since I was 17, playing in church and for wedding ceremonies, then onto solo gigs and with bands with my husband. My dream was one of those things I always saw as "just a dream."

But then I found Key West.

I will never forget my first day here. We were staying at the Southernmost Hotel, and decided to walk down Duval to the famous Sunset Celebration. By the time we were halfway down Duval, I was saying *I have to live here*…the shops, the diversity of the people, the smiles, the warm breeze…

I was in love.

When we reached Caroline Street, I heard music from the open doors of almost every bar, many of them solo acts, and I started saying *I have to sing here.*

And then we reached Mallory Square.

Everything I experienced there eventually became a song. I was fascinated by all the performers, but Will Soto's show touched me. I remember thinking that this person has been walking a wire for a living for 20 years, and I had never seen someone so happy to be doing what they love. Although music and wire-walking are far from similar, he was truly an inspiration to me, and for the first time I started to think that maybe my "dream" was possible.

I saw Will's show a few more times before we left, and other than a few brief words as I tipped him, we never met. After sunset we stopped in Capt. Tony's where a woman named Taz was playing, and I said *I want to play here. I want to do this.*

When I returned to New York, I could not get Key West out of my mind or my heart. All I could think about was living there and playing music there. I had never moved farther than an hour's drive away from my hometown (Binghamton, NY, to Ithaca, NY). I knew no one who lived in Key West, yet I was seriously thinking of moving there.

I kept thinking of Will's show, as well, and felt the need to start jotting down some lines, which inspired a tune in my head that became "From the Heart."

I told a few people that I was thinking of trying to move to Key West. My husband was supportive, yet doubtful. Our son was 20 at the time, a musician, as well, who was beginning to look at schools for sound engineering, leaning towards one in Florida.

We decided to return to KW again in November of 1997 to see if this was what I truly wanted or just a fantasy brought on by a cold, gloomy winter.

I had finished "From the Heart" in the summer of that year and decided to record it. I found Will's address online and mailed it to him.

In September he called me, and I was thrilled to find out that he loved the song, and invited me to play it at his show next time I was in Key West.

I told him I would be there in November, and that year I sang it while he was juggling at his show. Key West felt like home to me on that second trip, and I knew that the next time I came back, it would be to stay.

Back in New York State once again, I began making plans. I made a demo tape and promo packages and sent them out to several bars. I subscribed to the *Key West Citizen* newspaper. I was hoping to be in Key West by the summer, but a couple of deaths in my family put things on hold for a while.

But, I knew then, more than ever, that life was way too short, and I would regret this forever if I didn't give it a try.

My friends and family said I was either brave or crazy. I said I was both! I was just crazy enough to be brave, and brave enough to be crazy.

Surprisingly, everything started to fall into place. Through an Ad in the *Citizen*, I found a studio apartment and was "home" in Key West on September 10, 1998.

I then found a part-time office job and began to take more promo packages to the bars and talked to managers.

I went to Capt. Tony's several times and was told by a guy named Randy that he wanted to fit me into the schedule when there was an opening. My first gig there was December 10th. I was only playing a couple of shifts and filling in here and there, until one of the musicians left, and I began playing 4 days a week. I also picked up gigs at a few other bars, and was able to quit my "real" job in the spring.

I had written a few songs when I lived up north, but was so inspired by this island that I felt the need to put the magic into my music. I also completed a song about my grandmother that I had been attempting to write for 7 years, that somehow all came together in one night, on St. Patrick's Day, and became the title of my CD: "Legacy of Love."

It was recorded live at Capt. Tony's in 2001.

I gigged at Capt. Tony's for almost 10 years. There was a change in management, which brought about many cuts for musicians and bartenders. I was pretty devastated. It was 2008, and the economy was horrible to the point that many bars were opting for karaoke instead of paying for live music.

I sat in with Yankee Jack at The Bull that summer, and found a few scattered gigs, I then tried singing on the street for a year, which was humbling and horrible. By then, I was unable to keep my apartment and had moved in temporarily with Will and Amy, who have become (and still are) my best friends here. (I later found another roommate with whom I am still living). And then I decided to play where I first fell in love with Key

West…at Mallory.

I still play bar gigs when I can, and perform at the Key West Musicians Festival each year in September. It hasn't always been perfect. My marriage did not survive the move, but we remained friends until his death in 2010.

I endured and survived a nightmarish relationship, as well as a health crisis. Yet, through it all, I am still singing 5 nights a week at Sunset and so happy and blessed to be doing what I love."

AUTHOR'S NOTE: Key West gave Liz the confidence and courage to survive against all odds, and for that I have deep admiration for her.

You go girl!

CHAPTER 116—Clint Bullard

Al Subarsky told me that a few years back, he saw Clint playing (solo) guitar and singing at the Sunset Tiki at the Galleon Resort at the end of Front Street, just over there by A & B Lobster.

Alfonse listened for a while and liked what he saw, and he liked what he heard.

When Clint Bullard finished his set, Al Subarsky went up and introduced himself.

"Oh, I know who you are," Clint said. "Everyone on this island knows who you are."

Right off, Al and Clint clicked.

And Al suggested they join forces.

Al told me that "Clint is a fine songwriter/rhythm guitar/vocalist and my electric guitar work seemed to be a good match. He wore this cowboy hat (he's a proud Texan who spent quite a few years in Nashville), and I'm the Jewish guy from Jersey, so it was going to be a contrasting and fun duo.

But we needed a name.

"I needed to put my thinking cap on," Al said, "and since it was Key West, where's the best place to do that?"

"A bar?" I asked.

"That works," Al Subarsky said. "But actually I was lying out near the deep end of the pool one day and it struck me, and suddenly I had the name—**The Lone Star of David**! We played together for a good chunk of time, and it was really fun and well-received. We've grown from our experience together and have both returned to our respective solo gigs."

**AUTHOR'S where the heck is Clint NOTE: Clint Bullard plays every Sunday, Wednesday and Friday at the Sunset Tiki Bar & Grille at the Galleon, 617 Front Street.

See you there.

CHAPTER 117—????

Who am I talking about here?
He's outrageous.
Wicked.
Devilish.
Impish.
Colorful.
I could go on, so I will.
Hilarious.
Naughty.
Cheeky.
Sacrilegious.
Informative.
Committed.
And a right rascal of the highest order.

Yes, these endearing traits could only belong to that triple-threat persona in the form of our wild-mannered Gary Whitney Ek, known affectionately as the "Soundman From Hell" or the irreverent "Reverend Gweko W. Phlocker."

Gary produces, hosts, and rocks our world nightly on the radio at The X Key West 104.9.

And enriches our lives.

Tune in, people!

CHAPTER 118—Patrick and the Swayzees

Voted best band for the **2019 Bubbas: Key West's People's Choice Awards**.

The band is a hurricane of energy and entertainment onstage, and speaking of tempests, they have taken the local Key West music scene by storm.

This from the Green Parrot: "From surf rock to doo wop, rockabilly to beach music, Patrick and the Swayzees have created a current, yet still wholly nostalgic blend of early rock 'n' roll sounds that bring crowds to their feet from opening to encore. Their sets include original songs and instrumentals as well as a mix of well-known, crowd-favorite cover tunes, so there's something for everyone."

My kinda band!

But where did the name come from? I hear you ask.

"The three of us joked around using the word 'swayzee' as an adjective for 'sharp,' such as: 'That's a swayzee jacket.' Since we had a 'Patrick' in the band and we often dress up in bow ties when we play, we thought it was a funny play on words."

If a picture is worth a thousand words, then this video below from the Green Parrot is worth a gold mine:

https://www.youtube.com/watch?v=XPZHlxW1wKk

Have a peek.

It's swayzee!

CHAPTER 119—Dominique the Catman

Dominique LeFort has been performing in Key West since 1984, starting first at Mallory Square with his furry ensemble of "Flying Circus Cats."

This is where Gabrielle and I first met him.

Dominique would perform at the Sunset Celebration, Gabrielle and I were there flogging our framed Sunset Photographs and, just in case, I always had my Nikon at the ready endeavoring to capture the perfect photo of kitty-cat "Mars" leaping through the flaming hoop with a killer sunset kissing the horizon in the background, and Piggy, Spot and/or Sharky watching on from their stools, while they groomed.

"No grooming!"

Fast forward, and now Dominique performs regularly at Margaritaville Resort & Marina pier, adjacent to our legendary Sunset Celebration on the Mallory waterfront.

But how did he get all the way down here at the end of the world doing a comedy-enriched, lion-tamer act with house cats?

Dominique was born in Brittany, France, and grew up in the suburbs of Paris. As a young boy he wanted to be a clown, so he pursued a background in theatre: he studied drama in Paris for five years, opera for two years, mime at the famed Lecoq School for three years, and modern dance.

AUTHOR'S *"Fame!"* NOTE: "École Internationale de Théâtre Jacques Lecoq" is a school of physical theatre situated on Rue du Faubourg-Saint-Denis in the 10th arrondissement of Paris.

Geoffrey Rush went there—yes him from *Pirates of the Caribbean.*

* * *

Dominique eventually found work in Paris as a mime, but his goal was to work as a clown. Having said that, comedy in France is serious business and performing as a true clown is only reserved for "those who have lived life's experiences," not a young student who is just starting out, so he joined a theatre troupe and eventually made his way to Montreal where he performed his clown creation, the one, the only: "Rou Dou Dou!"

Then one day, Dominique mixed vacation with research and journeyed down to Florida to check out the famed circus scene in Sarasota. He also visited Disney World to see if any opportunity lay there. No go.

About now—and lucky for all of us—he heard about a unique venue in an enchanting part of the world: Key West's Mallory Square.

Dominique hit the road, aimed south down the Overseas Highway, arrived on the rock, and went right to Mallory that first evening.

And he was entranced by all the street performers entertaining at "Sunset."

What a grand venue for performers! he thought.

Back in Montreal, Dominique surprised his daughter Vanessa (who was three-years-old at the time) with a kitten named "Chaton."

"She pulled his tail, and Chaton came to me for protection," he says.

Dominique, who was still performing as the clown Rou Dou Dou, looked down at the now purring kitten and two big adoring eyes looked back up at him and POW! He was hit smack in the funny bone with the idea of incorporating a cat into his clown act.

But Montreal wasn't the right venue to develop and build a Cat Act, and Sarasota and Orlando were out.

But wait!

What about Key West?

And down at Mallory Square where EVERBODY was welcome?

So that's what he did.

Dominique stayed a year in Key West, tuning, tweaking and perfecting his act, and the act was such a grand hit, he ended up being "discovered" and hired to travel the country doing his cat shows. He traveled across the country from coast to coast and even eventually ended up playing Pleasure Island at Disney World.

But the venue at Pleasure Island was rife with too many distractions for his air force of Flying Cats.

What to do?

His heart was now beating loudly for Key West, so when he had fulfilled his contractual duties, he returned to Cayo Hueso and Mallory Square.

The purrrfect venue.

Nowadays, Dominique shares his Key West house with between seven and nine cats: the "stars of his show," plus the understudies and ingénues in waiting.

The training of a cat starts when it's a kitten, and can take up to a year for the little furry feline to be ready for the bright lights, or as is the case here—the setting sun.

"I do all the training myself, but the cats, they train me, to train them," he says laughing. "Sometimes one of the cats does something on stage that I think is good, so we keep it and make it part of the act. We work together."

And how does Dominique find just the right feline with innate stage-presence to be the next star?

"The cat must choose you, not the other way around," he says.

Just the way a cat likes it.

CHAPTER 120—Baby Tracy

That's Baby Tracy of The Fabulous Spectrelles Revue, of course.

Allison T. (Tracy) Mayer to those on the rock is the only remaining original member of "Divas of Doo-wop," the iconic international recording group that is Key West's longest running show at 35 years, and with Baby Tracy the longest-running female on Duval Street.

How about that!

If you happen to pass by The Bull at the corner of Duval and Caroline and see a large crowd standing outside the open front windows because it's wall-to-wall, whooping-it-up bodies inside, fight your way in, that's The Fabulous Spectrelles Revue up onstage!

Baby Tracy Spectrelle and Gabrielle Spectrelle will be kitted in short, TIGHT, sparkly dresses, and they're sexy, they're sassy, they're voluptuous. The third member is the talented Randy Riviera, and as a trio they really know how to whip a crowd.

I mean whip up a crowd.

The Fabulous Spectrelles Revue is a glorious tribute to the great girl groups of the 1960s such as The Ronettes, The Supremes and The Shirelles. If you fell in love with their style and their music, you will fall in love with the Spectrelles.

Check out The Fabulous Spectrelles Revue at LaTeDa (1125 Duval) in the Piano Bar, as well.

Go there.

Have a drink.

Have a dance.

Keep an eye on Baby Tracy's hips.

And be prepared to have you knickers blown off.

HEY, CHECK THIS OUT HISTORY BUFFS: I was talking to Baby Tracy and she was telling me about her mom,

"Betty Saint," who was a well-known jazz pianist here on the island. I HAVE TO INCLUDE THIS as it's just such a wonderful historical gem of family musical history.

This is **Baby Tracy Spectrelle** speaking now: "My mom's first gig was at a place called the Inner Circle lounge (at the old Key Wester, where the Beatles stayed). It was a big club here in the 60s. She also played at Two Friends with Bill Butler and Harry Chipchase and a drummer they called Chino. They were very well known jazz musicians here. Clayton Lopez or Coffee Butler would remember them. I think Clayton might be related to Bill. My grandmother also played keyboard, my grandfather played jazz and Dixieland clarinet and my aunt Terri played bass. My father was Capt. Bob of the famous Capt. Bob's Shrimp Dock restaurant on Caroline. He also owned The Lantern Inn Restaurant and Lounge where my mother played and gave many musicians their start. Skipper Kripitz and Marty Stonely to name a few. It is now Chico's Cantina. They would also play the Green Parrot. Jim Vagnini and my mother were in the Musicians' Union here together. My mother also played with Clayton Lopez later in life for the Blessed Community Gospel Choir that Clayton still sings in today. When my mom died all the musicians and the Blessed Community Gospel Choir gave her a procession and then sang at her funeral.

**TALK about music and entertaining being born in your blood, with that lineage Baby Tracy Spectrelle is blue-blood Key West royalty.

**AND the next time you're at The Bull or LaTeDa and you are enjoying Baby Tracy and the Fabulous Spectrelles Revue, take pause a moment and reflect upon what you've just read above…and it will help you understand the passion that Baby Tracy Spectrelle has for her group.

For entertaining.

And for Key West.

You rock, Baby Tracy!

CHAPTER 121—3 Local Heroes

I would like to honor the following three gentlemen.

They may not be celebrities, but they are heroes, indeed, and they deserve to be recognized.

And now will Danny Acosta, Henry Del Valle, and John Zeoli please stand up!

For those of you who have never heard these names, may I just mention (while we applaud them), that they are the talents behind the reparation and repainting of the Southernmost Point Buoy and "90 Miles to Cuba."

The iconic buoy was badly damaged when Hurricane Irma took a big bite out of it as 134-mph winds and waves lashed and sandblasted away not only the painted surface, but pitted and ripped at the underlying cement, as well.

First of all, John Zeoli, working like a sculptor, had to replenish and re-shaped the buoy with concrete on account of so much having been stripped away. Then he painted the basecoats to give the artists a canvas upon which to work.

Enter artists Danny Acosta and Henry Del Valle (who originally painted the marker in 1976), they then painstakingly brush-stroked in the detailing and the lettering.

These three men toiled relentlessly in difficult conditions to get the buoy back to its original state. Key West needed to get back up and running after the hurricane, so tourists would come and revive the shaken economy.

And the tourists wanted that buoy.

In the beginning, the Southernmost Point was marked with only a series of small signs, but all of them were stolen by irresponsible souvenir hunters, so the City of Key West erected something that couldn't be stuck in the trunk of your car, a four-ton concrete "marine buoy," 12-feet tall and 7-feet wide, *más o menos.*

The buoy was constructed over an old concrete sewer junction, and is arguably the most photographed attraction in the Keys.

As you may know, the Southernmost Point Buoy claims to mark the "southernmost point in the contiguous United States." In fact, Whitehead Spit, on U.S. Navy property just west of the buoy, is the true southernmost point, but cannot be accessed by civilians unless they're really drunk and have the required amount of bail on hand.

Check this out, Ballast Key is farther south:

Ballast Key Latitude: 24.5243° N

Key West Latitude:24.5551° N

Marquesas Latitude: 24.5754° N

Dry Tortugas Latitude: 24.6333° N

For those of you taking notes, the true Southernmost Point in the entire 50 United States is actually on the Big Island of Hawaii, in Ka Lae.

Ka Lae Latitude: 18.9136° N

And, more importantly, the nearest place to get a cold one is in Shaka's Bar, "the most southern bar in the U.S.A.," which is 14.5 miles to the north.

FY-hook 'em horns-I: The Southernmost Point in Texas in case you're wondering is near Brownsville, and it's called "South Point." South Point, Texas, Latitude: 25.8687° N.

Back to Key West: Next time you're down here and you're waiting in a life-sucking 20-minute queue to get that selfie of you and the Mrs. (or Mr.) in front of the buoy, turn around and have a peep at that cement hut right there behind you.

Yes, that one.

That my dear fans of history is actually a "telegraph" hut, and it was right here where a telephone cable entered the water and was strung all the way to Havana.

When did that happen, you ask?

I'm glad you asked: It was laid in 1917.

AFTERWORD

Well folks…that's it for now.

Apologies if I've missed anyone near-and-dear to your *corazón*. I will endeavor to include them the next time I'm riding my bike around the block.

I've presented you with some eye-opening scenarios here in this book and some delightful characters both temporal and permanent to the rock. Some of our celebrities made you laugh. Some made you cringe. Some we found to be more than just a little bit creepy, so let's bid this literary ship a sincere and rousing bon voyage and end with something innocent, warm and cuddly.

Ladies and gentlemen, boys and girls, all creatures great and small: I give you **CELEBRITY PETS!**

Dominique the Catman's Flying Circus Cats—The Hall of Pet Fame starts right here: Marlene, Mars, Spot, Piggy, Sharky, Oscar, Sara, Moon, Cosette, George, Hannibal, Jester, Mandarin, and Chopin.

Did I miss one?

Some of those feline stars of stage and screen have crossed over the Rainbow Bridge and are lighting up the heavens, jumping through the rings of Saturn now, others are still shining brightly each night, bringing laughter, wonder and joy to everyone from their youngest fans to their eldest admirers.

The show must go on!

And it will.

* * *

Bailey—Bailey, aka "Bailey Boo" to loved ones, is Al Subarsky's rescue pup. Well-known from the Jersey Shore all the way down to Key West, and an internet favorite, Bailey, with startlingly good looks, is the proverbial doggie-apple of Al Subarsky's eye.

This from Bailey's human, aka Alfonse: October 2015, I was on vacation on the Jersey Shore and happened to notice a post on Facebook by Cindy Kaye, who does dog rescue based in Sugarloaf, about 15 miles outside of Key West. The dog (at the time her name was "Sugar") jumped off the screen and I messaged Cindy that I would be back in town that following Monday and be at her place Tuesday A.M. to meet "Sugar"... She was originally found on the mean streets of Homestead/Florida City...in pretty poor shape. She was groomed, given all her shots, and sent down to Cindy's place with her paperwork. Maltese/Schnauzer mix, guesstimating 3-and-a-half-years young.

I drove up that Tuesday morn (Oct. 12th), she jumped in the passenger seat of my FJ Cruiser, and we headed back down to Cayo Hueso...she stared at me...I stared at her...and said "You aren't a 'Sugar,' but your name shall reveal itself!"

Next morning, I looked at her and announced: "You are Bailey!"

We went out, jumped in the truck, cruised around the block to Pet Supermarket, and had her name tag/I.D. made...and we drove into the glorious Key West sunset!

P.S. Bailey has been nothing but a sweet, loving joy since day #1.

**AUTHOR'S-Maltese/Schnauzer-NOTE: Bailey would say the same about her dad, Big Al!

* * *

"Crocodolly"—Crocodolly is not a Key West local—and certainly not a pet—but Crocodolly rocks a set of scales and deserves a mention.

Crocodolly was an eight-foot-long, female, endangered crocodile who had made the docks and canals around the bayside of north Plantation Key her home since 2010.

Most locals weren't too bothered, but some schmuck squealed and in came the big guns. Crocodolly was unceremoniously tagged (blue tag #5, BTW), and taken way out into Florida Bay and released.

But Crocodolly had put down roots in Plantation Key, so she said "Heck with this Florida Bay doo-dah, I'm going home!"

And she returned to her former habitat.

Everyone knew it was Crocodolly on account of the blue #5 tag on her tail.

Then she was re-captured and dumped farther out in Florida Bay.

But she returned again...to the exact same canal-side home with the fetching sun trap and the accepting locals.

Crocodolly was shy and respectful, and she always skulked quietly away when approached by humans, or simply looked on with innocent curiosity. She just wanted to get through another day being left alone and not causing anyone any agro, but Crocodolly was a growing girl and she was fast reaching the dreaded nine-foot barrier, deemed unacceptable by the FWC for squatting crocodiles.

So she was turfed out again and taken to a place far, far away, never to be seen again.

But guess what folks?

There was a reported sighting of our favorite #5 croc just last year.

Did she really return?

A few locals would swear in a court of law (not that you should ever swear in a court of law) that they spotted that fashionable #5 tag.

Perhaps Crocodolly is just like the rest of us, once she had a taste (so to speak) of the Florida Keys, she kept coming back.

The Keys disease.

Crocodolly is still a topic of conversation at watering holes (groan) up and down the island chain.

At the height of her popularity as a local celebrity, Crocodolly had her own Facebook page and over 400 friends. Which is pretty impressive, I would think, when you have short little arms.

AUTHOR'S PROUD NOTE: Gabrielle and I are Friends with Crocodolly on FB.

* * *

"Mr. Leroy"—is an alley cat (tropical lane cat) that adopted Gabrielle and me when we lived in Aronovitz Lane on the fringe of Bahama Village.

Mr. Leroy has risen from humble beginnings to become quite the literary celebrity on account of his starring, purring role in my KEY WEST SERIES.

Much like the great white shark in the movie *JAWS*, Mr. Leroy is a mindless eating machine. He has never met a morsel of food that he doesn't like. Black with a white moustache and white "spats," and therefore the very image of a well-dressed gangster of the '30s, he sleeps just above our heads at night, tiny, furry feet always touching one of us.

Mr. Leroy is the undisputed center of attention around our home/boat.

As he should be.

* * *

"Fausto"—is a rescue cat.

He rescued Popcorn Joe.

Joe named his beloved feline after Fausto's Food Palace on Fleming Street. Popcorn Joe first saw Fausto hanging out front of the grocery store one morning, then noticed the stray cat would follow customers into the market to the pet food aisle.

And then he would beg.

This was a cat that knew what he was doing!

Popcorn Joe adopted Fausto, and Fausto signed on with Popcorn Joe, and now they are leading a great idyllic life together at the end of the world.

* * *

Will Soto's Menagerie—Here's Will himself with us now to describe up close and personal his and Amy's menagerie…and it's a "Class Menagerie," I have to say.

Take it away, Will!

Thanks, Jon.

"Frodo" is a Min-Pin mix. He's the oldest and the alpha dog. He's 13 now and slowing down a little. Frodo came from the Marathon shelter (SUFA=Stand Up For Animals).

He's my "companion swimmer."

**AUTHOR'S COMPANION SWIMMER NOTE: If you have a peep at Will Soto's FB page, there's this hilarious pic of Will snorkeling through the mangroves. Standing on Will's back like Leonardo DiCaprio stood on the bow of the *Titanic*, is Frodo.

Frodo is cool!

"Henny Penny" is an eight-year-old Terrier mix. We got her from the KW shelter (SPCA). When I saw her she had a cone on so she couldn't lick or chew anywhere, so I asked 'Did you just fix her?'

The fellow at the shelter said 'No. She's been running in circles for two days chasing her tail. She finally caught it and bit it off. She's a bit psycho, and needs some love and attention.' I said 'Perfect. I'm like that too. We'll take her.'

"Cisco Kid" is a miniature rat terrier and the only pure-bred we have. Believe it or not, we got him when he was only six-weeks old from some guy at a yard sale who had just one left from a litter. I said: 'That's one of the cutest puppies I've ever seen.' He said: 'We sold the rest for $500 each, but we're moving to San Diego tomorrow. You can have her for free if you'd like.'

Cisco Kid is eight-years-old and in line to succeed Frodo as the alpha.

"Lilly" is a Heinz 57. A friend saved her from a kill-shelter in Miami. She's four-years-old and so full of pep and vinegar, that she keeps the other ones young by MAKING them play with her.

"REEF" is a five-year-old Calico, one-eyed pirate-kitty. We found her at the Marathon SPCA. She's as big as the dogs and RULES over them all. When we saw her at the shelter they said: 'She's pretty much un-adoptable. We've had her for a year. She doesn't like other cats. Hates dogs, and has bled several people that tried to pet her.'

Amy cautiously approached the grumpy cat, then turned and faced away from her. Eventually she started rubbing her head against Amy's back. 'PERFECT, we'll take her,' I said.

She bled us both at first, but eventually settled right in."

* * *

"Manxsie" is Johnny-Johnny's adorable Manx cat who has never had a tail and really doesn't see what the big fuss is all about if you do have one.

Like Johnny-Johnny, Manxsie is well-travelled, having started life on the Isle of Man (where the cat breed originates) in the Irish Sea between Ireland and the UK mainland.

Sometimes curt and demanding, Manxsie debunks that age-old principle that cats sleep 22 to 23 hours per day.

Manxsie could sleep more.

If it weren't for the eating.

* * *

"Sasha"—Sasha belongs to our friends Tina and Patty...or should I say they belong to Sasha.

You know how I showed you in a few of the above chapters the journeys that some folk had to take in order to end up in Key West and finally home?

Sasha is much the same.

Feast your peepers on *this* journey.

Sasha was an abandoned puppy, dumped, living under a bridge in Louisiana, endeavoring to avoid the scorching sun, alone, starving, sad.

Life just wasn't worth living.

Nobody loved her.

Nobody wanted her.

Nobody cared.

Then a kind woman happened to come along. We'll call her "Elizabeth," because that was her name.

Elizabeth spotted a pair of sad eyes staring out from under the bridge.

She approached the puppy.

The puppy cowered and backed up.

She held out a hand, cooed and coaxed.

The puppy retreated deeper under the bridge, quivering

with fear now.

There was no way the puppy was going to come out, and there was no way Elizabeth was going away.

It was a stalemate.

Time passed.

Elizabeth went to her car and pulled out some doggie biscuits. She always carried doggie treats with her wherever she went.

She approached the puppy again, sat down on the ground to be "small and non-threatening," and held the dog biscuit out in an outstretched hand.

The puppy's eyes locked on the dog biscuit like a smart-missile and its nose went into overdrive, but it didn't budge.

Elizabeth broke the dog biscuit in half and gently slid it closer to the puppy.

Nothing.

Elizabeth took the other half of dog biscuit and placed it even closer to the puppy, then she scooted a few steps back, all the while breaking up a few more dog biscuits and chumming a trail, just like "Elliott" did with the alien in the movie *E.T.*

"C'mon, little one," Elizabeth purred. "Don't be afraid. I won't harm you."

The combination of the soothing voice and the trail of broken biscuits was too much for the puppy to take and it took halting baby steps out from the shadows, tail curled tightly between its legs, and CHOMP, CHOMP, CHOMP, ate its way in the direction of Elizabeth.

The puppy came closer.

Elizabeth held out the back of her hand so the puppy could smell it and the puppy inch forward and LICKED Elizabeth's hand.

And soon Elizabeth was holding the puppy's face with both hands and caressing it and petting it and gently removing crud from its eyes and the puppy began to wail and wail and wail *COULD THIS REALLY BE HAPPENING TO ME!*

Elizabeth pulled out a bottle of water from the backpack she was carrying. She poured some water in the cupped palm of her hand and held it out. The puppy lapped at the water.

Elizabeth poured more water in her cupped palm.

The puppy drank greedily.

And Elizabeth caressed the puppy again. "You're just skin and bones and you're dehydrated…poor little thing."

Fast forward a few weeks, and Tina and Patty were down at Higgs Beach watching a loggerhead turtle being released back into the ocean after recovering at the Turtle Hospital, when Patty pointed back toward the seven bocce courts.

"What?" Tina asked.

"Not the bocce courts, next to it at the doggie park."

Tina shaded her eyes from the noon-day sun, and she could just make out a lot of frenzied activity. "C'mon," Tina said, "Let's go have a look."

Tina and Patty crossed over Atlantic Boulevard and entered the area of the doggie park.

A few owners were playing Frisbee with their dogs, a few others were throwing a tennis ball, yet a few others were just chatting with other dog owners as the dogs ran about playfully chasing each other, having the best time of their lives.

"There!" Patty said.

Off to the side of the doggie park were five puppies, different breeds, mixes, mutts, Heinz 57's, all frolicking about, tongues lolling. Suddenly, one of the puppies peeled off from the pack and ran right to Patty and Tina.

Patty and Tina knelt down and petted the puppy. Then they both sat down on the ground and the puppy jumped up in their laps.

"Sorry about that!" came a voice.

Tina and Patty shaded their eyes from the sun and saw a smiley woman standing there.

"She made a beeline for you."

Tina smiled at the woman. "Hi, I'm Tina and this is Patty."

"Nice to meet you," the woman said. "I'm Elizabeth."

And three hours later, Patty and Tina were back home on Geiger Key, sitting out in their backyard with the puppy playing at their feet.

"What should we call her?" Patty wondered out loud.

"How about Sasha?"

Okay, Dear Reader, the reason I recount this story is because Sasha has now turned six years old and has become a bit of a canine celebrity at the Geiger Key Marina Restaurant. She can be found holding sway there a few evenings a week, sitting right there between Tina and Patty's feet, happily snoozing, or just day dreaming about how wonderful life is when you have a forever-home, you're loved, and you have a family to look after.

KEEPING YOU IN THE LOOP NOTE:

Hey, you there!

Yes…YOU!

Keep this under your straw hat and don't tell a soul, but…Book #5 in my KEY WEST SERIES is in the works.

Yes, you heard right.

What?

You want to know what the title is going to be?

Okay, *whispering* now: **KEY WEST: Shrimper, Soldier, Sponger, Spy**.

You didn't hear this from me.

What?

What's that?

Now you want to know if all the usual suspects will be returning?

Okay, okay, okay, but you didn't hear it from me: Yes, Popcorn Joe is back, as is Johnny-Johnny, and John Rubin, and Mr. Leroy, and Manxsie, and Patty and Tina, and Al Subarsky…and a NEW character will be introduced called "Immo," a young curvaceous Cuban beauty with an angelic face and a devilish body who hangs out with Johnny-Johnny. "Immo" is a nickname for "Inmaculada Concepción." Her full first name is María de la Inmaculada Concepción—(Maria of the Immaculate Conception).

Yes, that is a fairly common first name in Spanish speaking countries—with such a long first name no wonder the gal needs a nickname.

It is rumored that Immo was a prostitute in Havana and has come to Key West to turn her life around. At the moment, it's not working, but lap dancing does pay well.

We're not sure if Immo is a bad influence on Johnny-Johnny, or it's the other way around.

Either way it's explosive.

And, nooo, I'm not saying Johnny-Johnny is her pimp. Why would you even think that? Huh? HUH?

As life sometimes throws you a curve, we get sucked in to the shenanigans (excuse the turn of phrase).

Immo is bent on living the American dream to the fullest, but she's currently still trying to pry herself out of the American nightmare that flourishes in Key West once the great clock on the corner of Southard and Duval has struck midnight.

Stay tuned.

We will keep you apprised.

So, once again Dear Reader, I bid you a temporary *adios!* And thank you for slogging through this book until the dog-eared end and not nodding off.

SIGNED: Jon, Gabrielle, and Mr. Leroy.

AND FINALLY:

I've been asked which is the best order to read my KEY WEST SERIES, (from the front of the book to the back of the book...I know *groan*) so here it is:

1) **KEY WEST: Tequila, a Pinch of Salt and a Quirky Slice of America**

2) **KEY WEST: Part II (the Seagull, I Mean the Sequel)**

3) **KEY WEST: Starting Over**

4) **KEY WEST: See It Before It Sinks**

Now beach fans, if you've read **Book #1**, look away now, but if you haven't, here is a wee peep into the start of the book for those of you who can't get to the bookstore and peel back the pages right then and there:

KEY WEST:

Tequila, a Pinch of Salt and a Quirky Slice of America

CHAPTER 1

The wind is deafening now. Howling. Screeching. This is Hades on earth and we are both terrified of the unknown. How long can this go on?

We peek out the crack in our boarded-up front window. The tree across the lane is bent sideways and coconuts shoot by like cannonballs. Why hadn't we evacuated when we first heard the hurricane was coming our way?

The wailing grows and grows and grows. Louder than before. Different than before. A baneful roar that is threatening to blow our house away. Then we hear a horrific splitting sound and there's a tremendous crash on our tin roof.

And our front door explodes open.

We rush the door and attempt to force it closed, but the hurricane fights back with unnatural strength. This monster is so relentless we have to lie flat on our backs and use our legs to wedge the door shut. As we're down there, frightened out of our minds and soaked to the skin, my life flashes in front of me. Curiously, it screeches to a halt at the part that got us into this mess in the first place.

* * *

"We don't care where it is," I said, glancing over at my wife, Gabrielle, "as long as it's south. Anywhere south."

The young lass working the desk at Barrhead Travel, in Glasgow, Scotland, giggled, squirmed in her seat, then tugged on the front of a blouse that was at least two sizes too small. Her name was Bridget, and she presented a sunny disposition on a crap-weather day.

"You'll be wanting the sun, then?" she said.

I glanced over at our brolly leaking all over the carpet. It was the first week of January. It had been pissing off and on for months -- since right near the end of the hosepipe ban.

"Sun is indeed what we're after," I said. "Shorts, tropical drinks with little umbrellas sticking out the top. That sort of thing. We'd kill for a really bad sunburn right about now."

Bridget hooked her hair behind her ear, shifted a copy of "Heat" out of the way and attacked the computer keyboard.

After banging away on the keys long enough to program the space shuttle, Bridget turned to us: "How 'bout Ibiza?"

Gabrielle gave me a terrified look.

"I fear we're too old for Ibiza."

Bridget assaulted the keyboard again and presented us with winter-sun destination number two: "Benidorm?"

"Too young for Benidorm in the winter."

"How 'bout Playa de las Américas?"

"Do either of us look like we're between 18 and 30?" I asked.

"Your wife does. You definitely don't," Bridget said candidly.

Gabrielle laughed.

"Magaluf?"

"Thanks, but no thanks."

"Playa del Inglés?"

I shook my head.

Bridget crinkled her nose at me: "Thought you said it didn't matter as long as it was south?"

"Did. Sorry."

Bridget consulted her computer again, then her eyes lit up: "Got just the place for you," she squealed. "You want sun. I've found you sun. You, Mr. and Mrs. Breakfield, are going to Key West, Florida. It's a tiny island at the end of the Florida Keys. I can get you a great fare, but you'll have to find your own accommodation."

"Key West! Don't they get hurricanes there?"

"Hurricanes?" Bridget laughed. "It's winter. Hurricane season doesn't start till June. Plus, they never hit Key West."

Then Bridget became serious: "But I should warn you about something. Key West may have an American flag stuck in the middle of it, but it's nothing like America."

* * *

Less than a week later, Gabrielle and I were sitting on an old cement dock in Key West, Florida, basking in late-afternoon wall-to-wall sun, our bare feet dangling down towards the Tanqueray-clear waters of the Gulf of Mexico. No stress. No cares. No umbrellas.

I had a beer in my hand that I had smuggled out of a nearby bar. Gabrielle had a margarita -- same modus operandi.

"Key West has serious wow factor," I said.

"Can't believe we're really here," Gabrielle said, smiling the world's widest smile.

A light breeze wafted out of Cuba. We could smell the salt in the air. It was 80 degrees. And the palm trees were doing the Salsa.

I quaffed my beer with great reverence. Gabrielle licked the salt on the rim of her margarita with deep sincerity. We watched as two local kids, brown as berries, fished off the dock for amber jack and mullet. The boys were about ten-years-old and they spoke in Spanish and laughed a lot. When it became too hot for the lads, they simply jumped into the sea and then climbed back up an old tire that was hanging over the side and used as a fender for docking shrimp boats.

What a great place to be a kid.

I pulled out our little guidebook. A colour map informed us that the entrance to the Key West Channel was just to our left, beyond that the coral reef and beyond that, only 90 miles from Key West, Havana, Cuba. As we sat there, letting the tropical air play in our hair and the sun warm our faces, the feeling was one of being at the end of the world. Last stop. End of the line. And nobody even knew we were here (except Bridget, of course).

And we couldn't imagine wanting to be anywhere else on earth.

HONNNK! HONNNK! HONNNK! An air horn sounded and Gabrielle shouted: "Look!" Off to our right we spotted an impressive yacht as it rounded the corner and slipped out of the harbor at the neighboring Ocean Key Resort. This was the glass-bottom boat and it was setting off on its daily sunset cruise. A boatload of delirious, palatic passengers waved wildly at us as the boat motored by. We waved back and toasted them with our drinks. And they all toasted back.

Sailboats cleaved the sparkling waters in front of us, a Coast Guard cutter came down the channel from our left and a vintage biplane pierced the airspace from the direction of the Key West airport and started doing loopty-loops.

We heard a curious plink-plonk sound and turned to see a bloke with dreadlocks playing a steel drum. Mallory Dock and the neighboring area known as Mallory Square was metamorphosing as various artists, street entertainers and musicians began arriving in rusted out vans, aging pickups and on funky bicycles.

What was this all about?

We dove back into the guidebook and discovered that in Key West, every day of the year, an hour or so before sunset, Mallory Square becomes a venue for the "Sunset Celebration": world-class street theatre, the sale of local arts and crafts, and the worshipping of the doggedly marketed Key West sunset. Were we ever looking forward to this!

Within an hour, the two little local boys had disappeared and beer-swilling grockles had taken their place. The less inebriated formed scrums around the engaging street performers. The pickled milled gooselike among the various craft vendors. And the hard-core drinkers sat in comatose bliss, staring out at the horizon, with now their feet dangling over the edge of the dock.

* * *

Gabrielle and I were watching a sailboat tack lazily in the direction of the setting sun, when suddenly she turned to me.

"Let's not go back."

"The hotel? No, we'll go have a whole lot of drinks first."

"No, I mean to Glasgow. Let's not go back. Let's stay here."

Gabrielle has a wicked sense of humor and I laughed.

"I'm not joking," she said.

I looked deep into my wife's eyes and they danced with adventure. This had been one of her qualities that had caught my eye when we'd first met. One of the reasons I had married her. She was exhilaratingly spontaneous and not at all afraid of a little adventure.

"Is it the margarita?" I said.

"No. I'm serious. Let's not go back."

"What about all our stuff?"

"Stuff it!"

"What about your job at the hotel?" I asked.

"They'll replace me with someone from France -- or Poland who speaks flawless English."

Gabrielle sipped her margarita, then turned to me with curious subtext. "What about your job at the airport? Do you like it?"

"Right, I leave in the dark and come home in the dark, and I stand there all day long talking to people flying off to exotic locales."

We turned our attention to an elderly Cuban fishing off the dock. The old man reeled in his line, checked his bait, then cast it back out into the aquamarine waters. He watched his line for a few moments with great interest, then sat down on an overturned bucket, opened up his bait box and extracted a cool Corona beer.

"Okay," I said. "Let's not go back. But what are we going to do for jobs?"

"What does it matter? We'll find something. You only live once."

"What about a car?"

"You obviously don't need a car in Key West. We'll buy

bicycles."

"What about clothes? We didn't bring much with us."

"It's a tropical island. How much do you need hanging in the armoire?"

"What about all our crap back in the UK?"

"Bribe family. There will be hell to pay until they realize they have a free place to stay in the Florida Keys."

This was all starting to sound pretty good, but then I thought of a problem -- a BIG problem.

"But you don't have a Green Card. You'll be illegal."

"I know," Gabrielle said, her eyes twinkling mischievously. "I bet there's hundreds of people working here illegally."

And what Gabrielle said right there in many ways summed up an aspect of Key West's spirit. It's a place where anything and everything goes -- plus some. And it's a far-flung island filled with hordes of foreigners and foreign intrigue. The perfect place to live if you are, say, illegal.

I grabbed Gabrielle's hand and we dove into the circus atmosphere that is Mallory Square at sunset. And with a frisson of excitement crackling between us (at least until the next day when we came to our senses) we strolled around this thrillingly colourful part of the world. And we couldn't believe what we saw: jugglers, fire eaters, a tightrope walker, musicians, a cat show, a dog show, a pig show, a bird show, a sword swallower, a guy whistling Amazing Grace, a gargoyle of a man galumphing about balancing a shopping trolley on his face and Statue Man. We also spotted troubadours, minstrels, a young demoiselle playing a violin and a gaggle of arts and crafts folk. There was even a fellow -- of questionable mental health -- weaving baskets, hats and lampshades (same size, same shape) out of palm fronds who went ballistic when an admiring soul innocently tried to snap his photo. And there were palm readers, Tarot card readers and psychics who professed universal peace and tranquility -- when they weren't at each other's throats for poaching business.

We fought our way through the sweaty bodies and down the dock in the direction of the Key West Aquarium where a little footbridge connects Mallory Square and the neighboring resort and came upon a group of tourists huddled at the edge of the pier. Everyone was staring down into the clear shallows. Holding sway was a deeply tanned, bare-chested entrepreneurial lowlife. This bloke was none other than "Fish-Man" and he was the equivalent of the fringe festival, an illegal performer who worked in the wings of the other entertainment by pointing out the brightly colored tropical fish cruising in and out of the pier. Simply said, he was a remora feeding off the nearby touristic frenzy.

We watched as Fish-Man threw his high-tech chum, which looked curiously like freshly buttered popcorn, down into the water to a flurry of darting creatures and then as they intercepted the fluffy white kernels, he rattled off his trophies: "There's a Slippery Dick!" All the women gasped as he pointed to a small tropical fish with a blue and yellow stripe that he obviously loved to open his act with. "And see that one there? That's a barracuda. And over there? Here comes a baby hammerhead! Begs the question: Where's mama?"

Everyone laughed.

Fish-Man pointed out a few more rubbery creatures, then suddenly wheeled on us, smiled an I've-been-sniffing-too-much glue smile and, as we all took a step back, held up an empty Pepsi cup for tips.

When no one would dare venture near him, he shrieked at us: "Goddamn fucking tourons! Why don't y'all go back up North!"

(We would later learn in Key West parlance a touron is a tourist/moron.)

Fish-Man drove home his sentiments with this colloquial barrage: "Any you sumbitches snag one of my pets, your corn-fed asses'll be grass and I'll be the lawn mower!"

It goes without saying (although say it I must), the crowd scarpered, scattering a flurry of peckish feral cats who had been peeping at the proceedings from the fragrant safety of a nearby jasmine bush.

As an experiment in subhuman behavior, I inched a few baby steps towards the now fish-eyed Fish-Man and held out a lonely dollar in my outstretched hand.

"Thank you, sir. Mighty kind of you, sir," Fish-Man said, snatching the buck with the charm of a moray eel. "Man's got to make an honest living. Got a narrow window for biz. When there's no sunset, I make no money." Then, he shot me a searching fish-eyed look: "Enjoy your stay. Just as soon have you here as some other asshole."

"I'll take that as a compliment," I said.

Suddenly a bagpipe wailed in the background, someone blew a conch shell and we all fell silent (Fish-Man put his hand over his heart) and watched, transfixed, as the sun squatted on the horizon and then melted over the backside of the earth.

It was a magical moment.

Everyone spontaneously applauded.

And I kissed Gabrielle.

What an exotic and undeniably unusual place Key West was.

Within a few minutes, as if higher powers were adjusting a dimmer switch up in the heavens, the sky began to slowly smear with ribbons of deep crimsons and rich magentas and lusty shades of cyan. In the distance, way out at sea, a towering thunderhead spit out shards of lightning and a low rumbling rolled our away. The gods were bowling (or moving furniture).

Then a loud scream. Now what! We swiveled around. A fight had broken out between the escape artist and one of the palm readers. The escape artist, in his lack-of-oxygen dotage, had apparently staggered on to the sacrosanct turf occupied by one of the palm readers, a crustacean of a woman with a comparable personality.

"She's going all postal again," came a friendly, amused voice from behind us.

We turned to see a cheery Elvis Costello look-alike pushing a mobile popcorn cart. His name was Popcorn Joe. A sign on Popcorn Joe's cart read: "Pretty Good Popcorn."

Popcorn Joe gave us a welcoming smile. "Just another day in paradise."

About now, a multi-generational family from the UK hurried up to purchase popcorn.

We watched Popcorn Joe in action. This was a man who knew his trade. And he really put on a show. As fresh popcorn spit out of the hopper, Joe flapped a white paper bag in the air, swirled a snowdrift-sized amount of popcorn around with an enormous stainless steel popcorn scoop, then excavated a prodigious amount into the maw of the bag: "That'll be three dollars, please," Popcorn Joe said, with a *Magnum, P.I.* fluttering of the eyebrows. "Refills and advice are free."

Three generations of family stood frozen in place, sunburnt faces aghast, mouths open like baby birds, regarding Popcorn Joe as if he were from the moon (or possibly deeper in the universe), then they smiled politely, paid for their popcorn and scurried off in the direction of the pig show.

Gabrielle motioned with her head towards the scampering family and whispered: "Grandfather's a Liverpudlian, son-in-law a Mancunian."

"Must be lively around the house on Saturday afternoons."

A phone rang somewhere. Popcorn Joe rooted through his money pouch and extracted a cell phone the size of a sea cucumber.

"Whaddaya need? How much? Tonight? Yeah, I think I can swing that."

"What was that all about?" I whispered to Gabrielle. "Sound as fishy to you as it did to me?"

"Didn't sound much like popcorn business."

Gabrielle and I took one more peek at the flaming sky, and the crabby palm reader who was trying to throw the chained-up escape artist into the Gulf of Mexico, then turned and hightailed it the hell out of there. We didn't want to still be around after dark.

Laughing, we fled Mallory Square by cutting in between the Waterfront Playhouse and El Meson de Pepe, a tropical outdoor bar/restaurant, where a Latin band was knocking out some *caliente* salsa and locals were throwing back shots of Cuervo. Then we turned left on a bricked alley -- called Wall Street -- and spilled out on to Duval Street.

We had read that Duval Street is the high street of Key West and it stretches from the Gulf of Mexico side of the island to the Atlantic Ocean side of the island, about one mile or so, and it is the spinal cord (and sexual organs) of the Old Town.

When you peregrinate and drink on Duval you are partaking of the famous "Duval Crawl" ("And bars to go before I sleep..."), and you will notice right off there is something here for everyone: fine restaurants, not so fine restaurants, T-shirt shops, strip clubs, semi-naked women ululating from second-floor balconies, gay bars, art galleries, cigar shops, T-shirts shops, illegal street performers, T-shirt shops, palm trees, time-share booths (masquerading as information booths), panhandlers, transients, did I mention T-shirt shops? henna tattoo booths, pulsing music venues, restaurant touts, pedicabs, mopeds, pink taxis, a python wrangler, a gentleman with an iguana on his shoulder (and iguana poop down his back) and a smiley, shaggy-blond-hair chap on a bicycle who resembles a tanned Boris Johnson.

Every conceivable square inch, every nook, every precious cranny, whether it be a crack between two buildings or simply an unused doorway, had a little flourishing business sprouting out of it. Talk about capitalism. We even saw a guy who had the world's smallest "Cuban" cigar business protruding out from a set of steep stairs.

Key West is indeed more Caribbean than it is American. And like the Caribbean, it's a place you go to learn to Scuba. And it's a place you go to enjoy tropical foliage, and island art and architecture. But it's also a place you go to get fucked up.

Duval Street was absolutely awash with paralytic revelers (walking about as sailors do on a rolling ship -- or on dry land, now that I think about it) and more of those Key West characters. Out in front of the Hog's Breath Saloon, and only about a block removed from Mallory Square, we happened upon a transient, with a lost-at-sea beard and hairy-knees, sitting on the curb. For some reason he seemed inordinately happy, in fact even happier than I am after the proctology exam is behind me for another year. The transient was holding up a sign that read: "Hell, why lie. I need some spare change so I can get drunk."

We kept walking and passed by a shop with a sign in it that read: BUY ONE, GET THE SECOND ONE FREE! It was a shoe shop.

Then we saw a middle-aged corpulent woman marching

down the street. She was wearing a T-shirt that read: "I have PMS and a gun. Excuse me, did you have something to say?"

In front of an entertainment complex called Rick's, a bony hand clamped on to my shoulder. I turned and stared into the wizened, weather-beaten face of someone I could only describe as a pirate -- a very polluted pirate (I'm a magnet to these people).

"Arrrghhh!" the pirate said. "My name's Captain Jerry. I'm the Wizard of Key West. Say, my friend, can I borrow thirty-seven cents?"

I was so taken aback by the requested amount, I immediately forked over a dollar.

We plunged back into the river of overheated bodies (it looked as if a football game had just ended) and were immediately set upon by a wag in theatrical makeup who bore a striking resemblance to the Joker in *Batman*. To present an air of vaudeville, the Joker was wearing sandwich boards.

"Hi! I'm the Joke-Man," he chortled. "Wanna hear a joke? Only twenty-five cents?" Then, very deadpan, "I've got cheaper ones, but they're not as funny."

Gabrielle laughed and handed over a quarter. Anybody with this much determination deserved the custom.

"My wife and I divorced over religious differences," the Joke-Man began, "I thought I was God, but she didn't." The Joke-Man laughed heartily at his own joke, then thanked us and accosted a family proudly wearing Green Bay Packers tops (away colours).

The crowd nudged us along at the speed continents shift. We peered into the window of a T-shirt shop. It featured T-shirts for infants. One T-shirt read: PARTY...MY CRIB...TWO A.M.

Laughing, we worked our way through an awful lot of people showing an awful lot of skin, up to the corner of Duval and Greene, and I thanked God we weren't going anywhere in a hurry. It was dark now and what a lovely night! Balmy, on the sticky side of muggy. Wind calm. Enormous moon rising. Heady aromas: night-blooming jasmine, bar smells, kitchen smells, body smells -- cannabis.

We stopped and looked kitty-corner across the street and right over there on the corner was none other than Sloppy Joe's bar (once the haunt of Ernest Hemingway). Just a block past Sloppy's, on the opposite side of the street, on the corner of Duval and Caroline, was a bar called The Bull & Whistle. The Bull & Whistle was an old wooden structure and it appeared to be made up of actually three bars: "The Bull" on ground level, the "Whistle Bar" one flight up and the "Garden of Eden" rooftop bar. The entire venue was old and funky and dark and moody, rough even, in an I'm-not-so-sure-I-will-come-out-alive sort of a way.

This was our kind of place!

We stepped out of the line of fire and gave the bar a good, hard look. All the windows were wide open and the joint was heaving. Up on stage, three thirty-something women with beehive hairdos and squeezed into tight, silver sequined dresses were belting out "It's Raining Men." Appropriate in a town with a large gay population. We were about to dive in when we spotted none other than Popcorn Joe. He was standing there on the corner with his mobile popcorn cart, working the Duval Street crowd.

We went up to Popcorn Joe. "You were just at Mallory Square."

"Very observant, masked man," he said.

"How did you beat us here?"

Popcorn Joe placed his hands at his temples as a swami would: "Let me guess. You took Duval, right?"

"Right."

"Duval was sardine-city, so I took the alley."

We hung out for a while and watched Popcorn Joe shovel popcorn and entertain the throngs. Joe seemed to know everyone on the street -- even the tourists. "Hey, how ya doin' Chris and Natalie? Nice to see ya again, ladies. Y'all stayin' long? Hope you left the kids at home."

When there was a lull in the booming popcorn sales, I asked Popcorn Joe about the three women singing up on stage inside at The Bull.

"They're the Fabulous Spectrelles Review. A Key West

institution. Been around for ages."

We listened as the Spectrelles sang "Y-M-C-A" (Gabrielle was miming the letters), then "Where the Boys Are."

"Check out the bar on the top floor," Popcorn Joe suggested. "You might find something of interest up there. Go around to the stairs on the side. You'll never make it if you try to storm the front."

We went around the corner on Caroline Street, sent a cat screeching into the night, and took the wooden outside stairs up to the Whistle. We stuck our heads in and the place was mobbed with a cast of characters who looked as if they had just stepped out of a Patrick Swayze roadhouse movie. Good-natured drunks were shooting pool, shooting the shit and shooting Alabama Slammers. Some were even hanging over the Havana-influenced, wrap-around, wrought-iron balcony watching the world go by below on Duval.

Two puckish scamps had a fishing rod with a large hairy spider attached to the end of the fishing line, and they were finding it good sport to let it drop down on the unsuspecting tourists—usually female. We observed for a minute, saw them drop the hairy beast down, heard a cacophony of primordial screams from below, saw them quickly reel the spider back in. Then they cackled and toasted each other with Killian's Red.

Not wanting to be party to such frivolity (read: frightened of spiders), we fled up another flight of rickety stairs to the mysterious Garden of Eden rooftop bar.

"Check out the bar on the top floor," Popcorn Joe had suggested. "You might find something of interest up there."

And you know what? Popcorn Joe was right. You see, the bar had a bouncer (the size of a refrigerator) checking IDs, but that was not unusual, what was unusual was the bouncer was a woman, and she was wearing a string-bikini bottom -- that was really more like floss -- and she was topless. And she was pissed as a fiddler's bitch.

Gabrielle pushed me towards the bouncing bouncer and Miss Frigidaire greeted me in a somewhat erotic, rather rural American I-can-suck-the-chrome-off-a-trailer-hitch manner and then gestured in the direction of the bar. How did this siren know that we suddenly needed a drink? A stiff one (I'm talking about the drink).

It was beyond dark up here in the Garden of Eden and when our eyes adjusted to the subdued lighting this is what we saw: We saw a young Cameron Diaz creature tending bar. She had false eyelashes like a Venus fly trap and was completely naked -- not even the floss -- and clearly a true blonde. And we spotted a DJ mixing tunes. He, too, was stark-buck naked. And we saw an artist. He was, get ready, *body* painting. And he apparently didn't want to get any paint on his clothes, because HE WASN'T WEARING ANY CLOTHES!!!

Neither did the guy who was having his body painted like a scene out of the original Garden of Eden, complete with the forked-tongue serpent. Or the fellow (hung like a racehorse) who was having his naked body painted like a pirate, replete with the golden dagger hanging from his sash.

Scotland this wasn't!

We peered into the dim light and cringed. Out on a dance floor, naked merrymakers were dancing to a very hump-me beat of a not-so-refined nature. In the wings, topless women, naked men and a few professional voyeurs of indeterminate sex were whacking back the bevy.

Key West was the epicenter of debauchery!

"Been to America before," Gabrielle shouted over the music. "Wasn't like this at the Magic Kingdom."

"They're having one helluva party down here and the rest of the world doesn't know it's going on."

The pirate/stud horse paid the body painter and hoofed it to the dance floor. I threw myself in front of Gabrielle to protect her so she wouldn't get accidentally flogged by Long Schlong Silver -- then I ordered a Budweiser and a margarita from Cameron Diaz behind the b-b-b-bar. Up close, Cameron had a rough look, but it was softened by a syrupy, seminal, phone-sex voice.

Not that I know about phone-sex voices.

No, really!

The feeling up here was one of being very far removed from the real world, the perfect place to come on holiday if you felt the need to get your mind off the backstabbing at work, the depressing side effects of your depression medication or that $80 parking ticket.

I inhaled my beer. And Gabrielle threw down her margarita. Then we did the same thing all over again. We were too embarrassed to stay -- and too embarrassed to leave.

Now what! A thundering commotion over by the bouncer suddenly rumbled our way. A group of young gays, naked except for G-strings and Nikes, had their bodies painted like zebras. They were coming in for a touchup -- and possibly a blow dry.

Jet lag was kicking in. We needed to go back to the hotel, but how were we going to escape from this bar? Perhaps we would make a move when the herd of zebras kicked up their heels.

Are you still there?

Schlemiel: "Someone who is not very intelligent or lucky and who is prone to making mistakes—often. A schlemiel goes around spilling soup on others."

Schlimazel: "An accident prone person. The Schlimazel gets the soup spilled on him/her."
Or to say it another way: The Schlemiel causes the sky to fall…but it only falls on the Schlimazel.

Hasenpfeffer: "Rabbit stew loaded with wine…so it doesn't taste like chicken."
I just thought you might want to know.

Printed in Great Britain
by Amazon